Shake, Rattle, and Learn

Classroom-tested ideas that use movement for active learning

Janet Millar Grant

Pembroke Publishers Limited

dedicated to my little bit of happiness,
Alexis Caitlin Grant

© 1995 Pembroke Publishers Limited
538 Hood Road
Markham, Ontario
L3R 3K9

Published in the U.S.A. by
Stenhouse Publishers
226 York Street
York, Maine 03909
ISBN (U.S.) 1-57110-019-9

Canadian Cataloguing in Publication Data

Grant, Janet Millar, 1960–
    Shake, rattle and learn

Includes bibliographical references and index.
ISBN 1-55138-049-8

1. Movement education. 2. Elementary school teaching.
I. Title.

GV452.G73 1995   372.86   C95-930319-7

Editor: Kate Revington
Designer: John Zehethofer
Typesetting: Jay Tee Graphics Ltd.

Printed and bound in Canada
9 8 7 6 5 4 3 2 1

Contents

Introduction

I love to watch children at play. I'm fascinated by the satisfaction that a sudden run can bring to them. I can feel the freedom of children skipping high and their surprise as they fall. I, too, delight in movement. I enjoy the energy of a brisk walk and the relief of an arm swing. We all revel in some form of movement. For most of us, however, movement is usually limited to outdoors.

If children love to move, why keep it outside of the classroom? Movement, regardless of where it happens, satisfies and energizes us. We can bring movement into the classroom or the gym and use the energy of movement to support learning. A balance of physical and intellectual activities improves students' overall physical and mental well-being and enhances academic performance. By bringing movement into the classroom, we will see an improvement in student discipline, academic performance, self-concept, independence and cooperation. Their skills in organization, planning, problem solving, imagination and creative thinking will also improve. As students learn through movement, we can use the motivation of movement to propel learning.

The lack of space or fear of students' bumping into desks need not be a concern. Movement-based learning can occur within the confines of a small lesson area on the carpet or even in the small spaces surrounding students' desks. Students working within limited space can be encouraged to control their movements so that they can move without touching any objects or any people. We can outline spaces in the room that can be used for movement and other spaces that pose safety concerns or that are out of bounds altogether. Students at all grade levels can successfully develop their spatial awareness and motor control to move through instructional strategies, reaping the benefits of the learning while confined to limited work spaces. Having access to a school gymnasium or empty classroom is unnecessary for most movement activities.

I believe that movement is essential to all children. They move to learn, to interact with people and to know objects. Children move throughout their lives, encountering many experiences. Movement is the vehicle through which they obtain experiences, express feelings, receive inspiration and develop concepts. Through body movement, children have life experiences and then respond to those experiences. Body movement plays an important role in the life and learning of children.

Our students should have a total education, and a total education includes movement. As students move through their day, they develop their cognitive, affective and psychomotor skills. Body movement allows children a way to combine feeling and thinking, a way to know the self and the world. The inclusion of a movement program in school would encourage students to develop a form of personal expression, learning and communication.

Movement is a means of learning. All students have specific learning styles, and students learn best through different forms, or a combination of forms of sensory perception. In order to meet the diverse needs of students, we should teach to a variety of learning styles, appealing to the use of different senses.

Kinesthetic learners are those who learn best while moving or while using the movement sense. Students respond to ideas they receive through movement. In the process, they understand how movement happens, what it feels like, and how to talk about the experience. The development of the kinesthetic sense allows students to increase their ability to use their own bodies in skilled and expressive ways, developing their abilities to receive and communicate information. These skills are necessary to the process of learning in all subject areas.

I wrote this book so that movement could break through outer walls and into all classrooms. Why? *Because movement can contribute to learning in all classroom studies, regardless of subject focus.*

Movement can become part of instructional strategies in all subject areas, demonstrating concepts to students in a concrete way. For example, movement learning-experiences can enable students to compare weight, size, shape and spatial relationships in mathematics. They can also promote learning about words, phrases, sentences, and poetry in language arts; rhythm, tempo, pitch and phrases in music; elements of design in visual arts; and levers, structures, magnets, and solutions, associated with science. You can apply the ideas in this book as alternative learning strategies to support classroom learning.

You will find that common concerns, such as how to introduce, control, monitor and develop movement in classroom activities, are addressed in each chapter. I have tested all classroom activities thoroughly, working with children from kindergarten to Grade 6; you may also see a wider application of the activities.

Each chapter focuses on a different theme that contributes to the introduction of movement into classroom activities. It outlines skills, movement content and extensions. The actual organization of virtually all chapters progresses from individual activities, to partner activities and finally to small-group, large-group, and in some cases, whole-class activities. References to literature as a potential stimulus are provided. Cross-curricular applications round out each chapter. *Shake, Rattle and Learn* presents richly textured, holistic learning experiences.

As you work through the nine, logically ordered chapters, or draw on them as resources for other courses, your students will have a chance to learn spatial, rhythm and music concepts, to analyze movement, to learn patterns, and to create logical movement sequences. They will learn the vocabulary of movement and will be able to discuss movement. They will also learn to control their bodies, develop a greater understanding of their feelings, express their thoughts and ideas, and construct knowledge.

Watch your students while they move . . . their faces, their bodies and their gestures. And as movement flows through your classroom, watch the learning of your students flourish!

Chapter No.	Primary Focus	Curriculum Connection	Key Stimuli	Learning Outcomes
One	story experiences	language arts	picture books personal experiences	Students will connect personal experiences and those presented in literature. Students will receive, process and communicate stories.
Two	environment	environmen-tal studies	sounds, book illustrations, nature	Students will gather and process information about the environment and interpret the information through movement.
Three	interpersonal relationships	guidance/ life skills	other students, story themes	Students will cooperate and collaborate to understand roles and relationships, especially familiar ones. Students will develop self-esteem and recognize the strength and importance of relationships.
Four	body communication	drama	words, phrases, sounds	Students will send and receive messages using the body as an instrument of communication. Students will interpret and respond to simple language. Students will respond as movers to conversations about words, phrases and sounds.

Chapter No.	Primary Focus	Curriculum Connection	Key Stimuli	Learning Outcomes
Five	poetry	language arts	rhymes, narrative and expressive poems	Students will interpret poetry to make the mood/emotion of the poetry concrete. Students will use the body to send and receive information.
Six	rhythm	music	rhythmic forms	Students will investigate elements of music such as tempo, duration and pitch. Students will explore, observe and record rhythm. Students will create simple movement sequences.
Seven	visual design	fine arts	picture books, lines, colours	Students will explore elements of visual design through movement.
Eight	spatial relationships	mathematics, science, fine arts	bodies, space	Students will demonstrate spatial awareness. Students will design three dimensionally.
Nine	societal issues	social studies	props, including a dancing stick, storytelling shawl, glasses, student art	Students will put themselves in another's shoes to pass on cultural history stories. Students will use props and movement to respond creatively to societal issues.

1 Experiencing Stories

Children love to share stories about their experiences: to talk about how they ride their bikes to school, took a family excursion to the zoo or built a snow fort in the winter. When you look at the pattern of children's stories, whether they are shared at a show-and-tell time or through general discussion, you'll see that many stories relate to activities in which children participated physically. These tales are shared with zeal and enthusiasm.

In the process of learning, students must make meaningful connections between personal experiences and the world around them. In order to do this, they need concrete experiences through which they can physically receive, process and communicate information. Movement activities involve the body experiencing the world, leading to understanding and learning.

As teachers, we seek to make links between the children's world and curriculum content. We want to make obvious the connections between students' experience and new knowledge, skills and attitudes. If that happens learning will result.

Physically experiencing new ideas and concepts helps students to form those learning connections. The use of physical activity as a method for receiving, processing and communicating learning can be applied to all areas of the curriculum. Indeed, the physical self can bring understanding to any arena of learning.

In this chapter, children begin by experiencing stories, receiving, processing and communicating them. They can select, interpret and produce scenes from books and their own experiences. Through a physical response, they will also have an opportunity to focus on their favourite part of a book, re-create sections of a book and retell a tale through dance. At the same time, you can take a focused look at story elements, characters, events and plot.

For the activities in this chapter, you can use any favourite classroom picture book. Books that are explored within this chapter include *We're Going on a Bear Hunt, Stringbean's Trip to the Shining Sea, Travels for Two, The Mysteries of Harris Burdick* and *The True Story of the Three Little Pigs*. I selected books that outline personal travels or adventures. Once you have made your selection, you are ready to begin!

Moving Through Story Scenes

Journeying Through Story Scenes

This movement activity takes children through the scenes of a journey and invites them to accompany a story rhyme with movement. Children will learn about story scenes, rhythm and tempo and develop their ability to select movement for a story.

You need to choose a storybook with a repeating pattern or rhyme, preferably with a combination of black-and-white and colour illustrations. One book that works well is *We're Going on a Bear Hunt* by Michael Rosen. The strength of this version lies in the illustrations by Helen Oxenbury. The pages alternate between the black-and-white illustrations of the pattern *we're going on a bear hunt* and the full colour of each action.

With the class, make a list of the scenes you find in the book you choose. Your list may have headings such as the following:

- swishy swashy into long wavy grass
- splash splosh across the deep, cold river
- squelch squerch in the thick, oozy mud
- stumble trip in the big, dark forest
- hooo wooo in the swirling, whirling snowstorm
- tiptoe tiptoe into the narrow gloomy cave

Now, students are ready to join the book characters on an adventure. Ask students to remain still during the black-and-white pattern pages, and to move during the coloured pages. Students can move on the spot using whatever movement comes to mind. They may be reluctant to move at first and use only small foot movements, but as the journey continues, they will use a wider range of arm, leg and torso movements.

In my classroom, we also enjoyed exploring the book scenes of *We're Going on a Bear Hunt* in character roles. For the role of the baby, the movements were tentative and underdeveloped, always reaching and becoming quickly tired. The boy used his stick to help him, but sometimes felt that it weighed him down. Each student in the class selected one of the roles and moved through each of the coloured page scenes in that role. We then discussed how our impressions changed with the whole class.

Extending the Activity: You might invite your students to consider what could happen to the book characters at the end of the story. You could ask students to record their endings by drawing pictures. Once all of the pictures are finished, students can meet on the carpet to retell the stories with the new endings. I found that some students climbed a tree and one even ended up on a rooftop!

Storytelling Personal Experiences

This activity encourages students to look at the events in their own lives. Your students will learn to communicate personal experience stories through movement.

For students, every day is a sequence of events and experiences that happen as they wake up, eat at the breakfast table, ride on the school bus, play on the playground, enter the school, and have lunch. Before beginning this activity, you might choose to discuss with your students their daily schedules. I've known children to slip and fall, get lost or plan recess games with a friend on the way to the washroom alone! Any story that chronicles daily routines, such as *Travels for Two: Stories and Lies from My Childhood* by Stéphane Poulin, can be used to generate additional discussion on personal experiences.

Children can tell a story of those personal experiences by looking at them in three parts: what happened before, during and after the event. For example, I started off on my way to school in the rain, a car drove by and splashed water on me, and I was dripping wet all day.

Start by asking your students to focus on a funny thing that happened to them. Once all of the students have had time to think, ask them to take a body shape to show how they were just before the event, capture their experience of the event through an action or movement, and freeze in a body shape at the end of the event. Your students can repeat the process for several other types of events such as these:

- a sad event
- a serious experience
- a frightening tale
- an adventure

In my classroom, once students had developed their movement phrases, they were eager to share their stories with a friend or in small groups of three. After they had done so, I divided the class in half and had the groups alternately share their movement stories with the remainder of the class. I challenged the watchers, each of whom focused on a different mover, to discover the stories in the movements. I also invited them to ask questions of the movers to clarify their understanding.

One student began his story with small relaxed movements of the arms and twists of the torso, suddenly expanding into jutting arms and legs and leaping to sudden quick movements in many directions, through calm, then vibrant and manic movement. It was through these movements that the student told the tale of his father barbecuing in the backyard when the food on the grill caught on fire and the family panicked.

Extending the Activity: You can encourage students to look at their own writing as a source of personal experiences. They might choose from their own print stories, published tales or journal entries. "It happened to me" could be a book with the author's picture on the front cover, the print outlining an important, interesting or amusing event that happened to the student. You might want to encourage children to provide more detail in their personal writing by having them "move" the printed story with a beginning shape, a middle movement and an ending shape. Then you could give students a chance to sit down and add description to their written tales.

Capturing Book Characters Through Movement

Students can learn much about character development by examining and role playing specific characters. In this observation and role-playing activity, students analyze and portray book characters. In the process, they will learn to observe characters and understand character development and presentation.

You can introduce this activity by reviewing with the class a book that highlights characters. I have found that *The Shrinking* of *Treehorn* by Florence Parry Heide and *Grandma's Secret* by Paulette Bourgeois both work well. With the class, make a list of the characters you find in the chosen book. The children will need to look closely at the illustrations and descriptions to find more information about the characters. Ask them to identify traits for each character. You might find some of the following questions helpful in generating discussion:

- What facial expressions do they often use?
- How are their backs as they are standing?
- Where are their hands?
- What body shapes do they take when they are listening to someone?
- Does this change from person to person?
- How do they move?
- Do they move slowly or quickly?
- Do they bump into items, or move with control?
- What do they like to do?

Now they're ready to begin. Invite your students to select a character. Then, in their own work spaces, have them explore different body shapes to portray that character through movement. Students can portray their chosen character through a still shape or a traveling action.

Let students share their movement portrayals with the class. I found that my students enjoyed the challenge of identifying each character presented through movement. Many of the students chose to represent the Treehorn character. The gradual shrinking of his shape was fun for the students to experience, while his posture also became more and more rounded and dejected. Many students portrayed this character with a confused look on their face, jumping up to talk to others and to get a drink of water.

To conclude this activity, you can revisit the book with students moving as their chosen character moved within the story. Have students remain still in a shape when their book character is still.

Extending the Activity: You can invite students to write a story about their character in a Character Book. Students can describe the character and outline what happened to the character, where the event took place, and how the story ended. Students can even create a dance to bring their character to life! Children might choose to put their finished story into a Shape

Book that captures their own character. One of my students chose to create a very small book, cut in the shape of Treehorn.

You might want to develop a bin collection of "action-based" stories for children to sit down to, then move to, to enjoy! Students can select story characters from such sources as anthologies, picture books, chapter books, personal stories and journal entries for movement portrayal. You might want to provide opportunities for students to share their discoveries with a friend. **Resources**, at the back of this book, may help you in your creation of a story book bin.

Entering a Story with a Partner

Showing the Best Part

The best part of a story will vary from child to child, but will always awake excitement and vivid imagery in the reader. In this activity, partners work together to re-create sections of a familiar story. The children will learn to use movements collaboratively to identify, develop, refine and express their favourite book image.

Many books outline children's adventures and journeys. One of my personal favourites, *Stringbean's Trip to the Shining Sea*, captures a child's adventures on postcards as he takes a trip across country to the Pacific Ocean. No matter what the chosen book is, have students work in pairs to identify their favourite section. Once asked, students are eager to share their images in movement and in words.

Ask one student in each pair to act out the chosen part for the partner. Students should depict the beginning, middle and ending of the story section with a start shape, a traveling action and an ending shape. The partners can then ask questions for details and understanding while the mover answers with movement. Have students change roles, taking turns as presenters and movers.

When we tried this activity in my class, one partner played Stringbean swimming in the lake, splashing and kicking, dropping under water as the other partner (Potato) landed on him, and then rising to the surface, laughing and sputtering with happiness.

18

You might want to ask the partners to put their best parts together to form a Story Dance. I found that the children need to decide whether to move for their own section, or for both sections. The children also need to determine the order of the sections and how to join the sections for a logical flow, both in story and in movement.

Extending the Activity: Invite the children to choose a paragraph or section of a story they would like to re-create in pairs through movement. I found that students did a particularly good job using action scenes, with walking, running, leaping and jumping. Challenge students to capture the excitement of their section by exploring time in fast and slow movements. Students might choose to share their best part with the class.

Exploring Story Scenes in a Group

Moving Right Along

To encourage students to explore the movements of a character, scene or event, you might want to introduce this group action/reaction game. Children will develop their communication and connecting skills as they receive, process and produce connected movement around a circle.

Have children stand in small group circles. Ask one child to begin with a movement, such as a stretch, a bend, a quick jump, a slow fall, a shoulder movement, a tricky turn, a leap, or a low run.

Then, have the next child in the circle repeat that movement, and add a new movement. Repeat this process around the circle, with each person adding a new movement to those movements being passed around. In this way, movement "ripples" around the circle until all children in the circle have added a movement. By the end of the sequence, there should be as many movements as there are children in the circle!

In one group I worked with, one student began with a twitch; the second repeated the twitch and added a small jump; the third did a twitch, small jump and head roll; and the fourth did a twitch, small jump, and head roll into a slide. You can encourage students to try to repeat their movements low to the ground, or have them try to pass the sequence in reverse order, beginning with the last movement and working around the circle to the first.

Extending the Activity: You might use a game to explore characters. First, assign one character to each small group. Beginning with a designated person in the circle, the children in the group should pass every character movement around the circle, each person adding their own interpretation to the collection of movements.

Repeat the activity with different characters, or share each of the group's character interpretations with the rest of the class. Students begin with the obvious characteristics, but the last few students must depict less obvious movements, such as the droop of shoulders, or the slight pause in a walk.

We tried to place the character into a scene by extending the movements to convey both character and background. Each group discussed the setting for their movement sequences and the character's reaction in the scenes. I found that students could "move right along" with the scenes as they pass the character around the circle, leading the character through long grass, a dark forest, the dry desert . . . and responding as the character in movement!

Retelling a Tale Through Movement

You may enjoy this retelling activity as a way to gain insight into the mechanics of a story. This activity involves students in sequencing story events and examining the perspectives of characters and the causes and effects of events in the story. Students will learn the process of story development and the skill of retelling a familiar tale.

There are several children's books that present a traditional tale from a different perspective. I chose to work with *The True Story of the Three Little Pigs* by Jon Scieszka. Once you have selected a book, you'll probably want to discuss its sections and list story aspects or events on chart paper or some other form of information organizer in your classroom. Your gathered information may reflect the following questions:

- Who is the narrator?
- Which events happened at the beginning, in the middle and at the end of the story?
- Where do the events happen?
- When do the events happen?
- What are the causes and effects of the events in the story?

Now that the class is ready to begin, you can ask each group of children to identify a section of the story that they would like to depict and a narrator to provide the spoken thread to draw their movements into a unified whole.

Each group can then work on depicting the beginning, development and conclusion of their section through movement, incorporating a combination of body shape and movement with stillness in the portrayal. I found that each group took some time to select and refine their movements into a familiar sequence, while the narrator was busy selecting and refining the words to be spoken. My students found that the narrator's role was very important, since the narrator's words triggered the movement phrases.

Once students have selected and prepared their movements, they should stand ready. You might choose to take the role of time keeper and decision maker, indicating which group begins by clapping hands at that group. The beginning group tells the story through movement to the accompaniment of the words of their narrator. This group can continue until you signal the next group to take over. You can repeat this process until each group has had a turn and the whole story is portrayed.

We had a lot of fun making a narrated dance about the Three Little Pigs. As time keeper I found that I had the flexibility needed to provide each group with enough time, yet maintain the pace of the whole presentation. The students responded with a wonderful dance and we used this approach again with other familiar tales such as Rumpelstiltskin, Cinderella and Pinocchio.

Dancing a Story

You might want to suggest that the children capture an aspect of a story in dance. Students will identify themes, events and motifs and address a story's theme through movement. They will learn to access story components, clarify focus and solve problems as they create a movement story.

You might want to entice your students with a specific story genre, such as mystery books. I found that *The Mysteries of Harris Burdick* is a good source of mystery story material. With the class, you'll want to discuss the unanswered questions in whatever book you choose and create a list of these puzzles. Your list may include:

- Where did they go?
- Why was that done?

- Who was there?

You can beat out a series of eight counts and have the children experience moving for eight counts, and then stop for eight counts. You might want to use a rhythm instrument for this beating: a simple hand drum, rhythm sticks or a tambourine. Or, have the children beat out their own counts.

Next, challenge your students to move for eight counts in one character, then change to another character for the next eight counts. You can lead their characters into different experiences and scenes, a different one for each eight-count phrase. Continue in this manner until students develop a feel for the phrasing.

For the next section, the students may enjoy working in small groups. Ask each group of students to select one event that they would like to address in movement for the dance. Those groups then work to create a dance that is eight counts long about their chosen event. The sequence should explore the problem and should have a beginning shape for all dancers, include a variety of traveling actions, and have an ending shape. You can remind students to consider different characters in the story and how they could represent them in movement.

When working with *The Mysteries of Harris Burdick*, one group in my class chose to represent *under the rug* with all students beginning in small tight shape, traveling low to the ground and ending in a huddle formation. Another group, whose problem was the sending and returning of the rock, dealt with the problem by pulling their starting shape, showing elastic movement to and fro across the space and using continual movement, even within the ending shape.

You could review the order of the events in the story with the groups and thus the order of the events in their dance. Then the groups can run through their dances to the accompaniment of the rhythm instrument. Watch for the clarity and suitability of the problem in the movement of each group.

Across the Curriculum

• Art: Creating a flip book or accordion book

Children can capture dancers "in action" in a picture book. They might want to try to create a flip book based on the shapes and movements observed in the dancers, a different shape on the edge of the paper, slowly changing shape and form so that when flashed through there is the appearance of movement.

Alternatively, students could create an accordion book. An accordion book consists of a series of panels that unfold to tell the story. Each panel can depict one of the story's scenes.

How to Make Pop-ups by Joan Irvine may prove to be a good resource.

• Art: Cutting Stories

Figures can be drawn ahead and cut out as the story is told.

• Music: Writing and tape-recording a story ballad

You could invite students to write and record their own ballads, telling their tales through lyrics and music. Students can use rhythm instruments to create the instrumental base and then incorporate action words, character sketches and scene descriptions into the lyrics. The end product can even be recorded live on audio tape and used later to accompany dance segments.

• Drama: Creating a script

Each group can script the spoken parts of the dance. This script may take on a variety of forms:

- the narrator's words describing the dance
- the narrator speaking the words of the other characters
- the characters' words spoken as they move
- the characters' words spoken at intervals during the dance by each character

• Language Arts: Collecting movement stories, recording dances, responding in journals

Encourage the children to create their own collections of movement stories, perhaps developing a class collection. Have each student bring a favourite book and record their observations about the characters, events, sequences and favourite parts in their journals.

You could have your students record their dances in words, setting description, scene, character description or symbols, and begin a class dance book collection for pleasure or for use in presentations.

2 Exploring and Interpreting the Environment

Children are surrounded by a world full of pictures, objects, and natural phenomena. Their lives unfold against the background of the world around them, and the world has an impact on their daily lives. Children need to explore the environment in their ongoing daily activities: to see the patterns in the environment, to describe their surroundings, to determine the attributes of the objects around them — the shape, thickness, colour and texture of objects. By physically capturing and perhaps re-creating, children can develop a personal connection with their immediate world.

This chapter allows children to develop a physical knowledge of the environment. Students will observe aspects of the environment through pictures and illustrations, processing that information and finally interpreting it through movement. They will also draw on other senses, such as hearing, to better understand the environment. Students can develop the skills of selecting, receiving, processing and interpreting which are necessary to all areas of learning that involve gathering and processing information.

All chapter activities focus students on developing observation skills for use across the curriculum: through their physical activity, students analyze, evaluate and represent the environment. Students will observe the environment in pictures and capture the pictures in movement shapes. They will bring illustrations to life, interpreting their design elements, such as rhythm, space and texture, through movement. They will also interpret changes through changes in body shape, individually and in pairs, and create pictures with sounds, group soundscapes and sound stories.

Countless pieces of literature can be used to support this exploration of the environment. In this chapter I have selected books with rich illustrations and those that present a variety of illustrating techniques. I have used the focuses of these books in a variety of ways to observe and interpret the environment.

Looking at Environmental Pictures

Responding Physically to Book Illustrations

This activity involves students in looking at pictures of the environment and moving in response to what they see. Through it, students will develop their receiving skills as they locate, select, focus and interpret information through movement.

To interest children in aspects of the environment, you may want to select a book with an environmental focus. *The First Forest* by John Gile is a tale of how the first forests came to be. I found this story works well.

With your class, focus on your book's illustrations. Encourage the children to consider how the pictures make them feel and how they can capture those pictures in movement shapes. In my classroom, we made the following list:

- a cluster of trees in the winter, some deciduous and others evergreen
- different types of leaves and fruit representing different trees
- trees in their youth, trees of many shapes, sizes and colours
- same grove of grey and aging trees, broken, fallen and diseased
- evergreen glade that had remained untouched

Next, it's time to begin the activity. Invite your students to move on the spot to convey the pictures as you read the book, but tell them to freeze in a shape as each page is turned.

My students' movements captured the wavy ripples of water and the squiggle of the colours. Some of the students depicted objects, while others showed aspects of the objects in space. At first, all students worked at a standing level, but as they became more aware of the details of the pictures, they changed their body shapes and levels. I found that capturing all of the changes to the illustrations without spending more time on each picture was difficult. So, we revisited the book. This time, each time I turned the pages, students read the pictures from left to right through constant body motion. Doing this really helped the students develop a greater flow to their movement and helped to move them toward improvisation with a wider range of movement.

Extending the Activity: Invite the children to play the running game of Trees. Have all students at one end of the room and a lumberjack standing in the middle. As the lumberjack calls "Trees," the students try to run to the other side of the room. Those children touched by the lumberjack grow roots right where they are and become trees. The next time the lumberjack calls "Trees," the trees and the lumberjack try to touch the runners. The game ends when the room is heavily forested.

Physically Creating Pictures

This activity heightens students' observation skills. Students change shape in response to the changing shapes of presented illustrations. In the process, they learn to attend to detail, concentrate and focus on task and respond to change.

You can begin with a book in which the pictures gradually change from page to page. *Changes* by Anthony Browne is a magical book in which the objects within the pictures do change from page to page. On first reading, you can direct the students to watch to see how the pictures evolve. Once you have read the entire book, you might choose to discuss the changes with the class. The children find the activity so exciting that they can't help but call the changes out as the pages turn.

Now the movement begins. Encourage the children to select an object from the first page of the book and to take a beginning shape for that object. Then as each page turns, your students can change their shapes as the illustrations change.

In my classroom, one student began in a rounded shape, slowly extended two limbs for ears, and grew a tail as his body grew and grew into a cat shape. I found that many of my students used a limited range of movement until I challenged them to look at the size and range of objects on the page. I also found that the children benefited by discussing each illustration to identify what might have happened before, during and after the picture. For example: For *before*, children suggested sitting in a chair shape; *during* would be extending arms; and *after* could be the emergence of a gorilla.

You might want to challenge the children to move and freeze

for each frame. To help the transition from before to during and after in locomotor movements, I have used a hand clap for before, a double clap for during, and a triple clap for after. Students should focus on achieving a smooth and sustained flow from shape to shape.

Making Pictures in Pairs

Playing with a Shadow Partner

Encouraging your students to engage in a shadow game will provide them with an interesting learning experience. In it they can take turns, lead and follow, communicate and develop a variety of movement. You might choose to introduce the activity with a book, such as *The Boy with Two Shadows* or *Me and My Shadow*, or go directly outside on a sunny day.

Once you are outside, you might want to challenge your students to find their shadows. As they work on the spot, ask the children to create different shapes with their bodies and watch to see the shadow response. Your students may choose to try jumps, leaps and other large movements on the spot, still watching their shadows. Once they tire out, you may want to discuss with your class how their shadows moved and what size, shape and image they had.

There are so many ways to work with shadows. Encourage your students to try some of these activities:

- playing tag with their shadows
- jumping on their shadows
- moving from big to small movements, and reversing
- leading with different body parts

Once my students had a chance to explore, they worked on their own to select and refine a sequence of two movement phrases of "Just Me and My Shadow." We had to work quickly to finish the exploration and share creations before we lost the sunlight and their dancing partners.

Extending the Activity: You could introduce mirroring and following. Invite the children to present their movement phrases to their partners and have the partners mirror their phrases. Then the partners can change roles. You can try having the reflecting begin a few seconds after the first mirroring, so that the movements are the same, but one after another.

Creating a Living Environment

Creating a Soundscape

Children love to play with sounds. In this activity, students listen to and select sounds and movement words, and then work in groups to dance a nature study. Students involved in this activity will develop their skills of listening, selecting and sequencing, consolidation and presentation.

Rain Drop Splash by Alvin Tresselt serves as a good source for sounds and movement words. Many other books or sound recordings built on a nature theme would also work well for this exercise. To prepare for movement, you might want to have your students imagine what they might hear if they were placed in a given setting, such as a river bed, a ravine lot, a conservation area or wetlands. Some of the sounds that my students imagined included the gurgling water and the screeching of the gulls over the sound of the rain.

Once your discussion is focused upon nature sounds, you can work with your class to create a chart. This chart should list the source of sound and the sound created, a way to create the sound, and the movement of each sound. Your chart might look something like this:

Object	Sound	Movement	Accompaniment
bird	chirp	jerky, hopping	kinds of whistles
insect	buzz	soaring, stop and go	voice
rain	patter	quick, sharp	wood block
water	rush	leaping, tumbling	wire brush on drum
wind	howl	swirling, irregular	voice, soft rubbing
fire	crackle	leaping, rising	cellophane to crunch

Let your children select an object that they would like to explore. Once they have identified one, you can ask them to find a way to make the sound, which may be the way listed on the chart. Working with the sound accompaniment, each student should develop a movement phrase to describe his or her object.

Once your students can really remember their movement phrases, they might want to join with other students and put their movement phrases together to form a danced nature study.

Extending the Activity: Some of your students may want to record their sound creations. You might want to encourage these children to create symbols to represent their objects, sounds and movement phrases. The symbols can then be used to record the order of the movement phrases within a group. One group in my classroom used this technique to help them keep track as they played around with the sequence of the movement phrases.

Making Sound Stories

To encourage students to examine their environment and record their impressions, you might want to do this sound story activity. I have done it with primary students, but you might find it works best with Grade 4 and up. The children will learn how to isolate, record and reproduce sounds, and in the process, understand their environment more fully.

To begin this activity, you'll need to select a scene from the environment. You might choose to do this by taking a walk through the school playground, a woodlot or past a local pond. Or, you could choose a scene from a richly illustrated book, such as *The Widow's Broom*. Ask your students to form groups and select a scene which they all want to work with. When my class worked with *The Widow's Broom*, some students chose the white handled broom carrying an axe in the forest, the broom sweeping, and a witch astride the broom.

Next, have each group of students identify sounds to accompany their scene, and create an audio tape. They will probably need some time to find objects to make the sounds: those of creaking doors, howling owls and snapping branches. Ask the children to create a 30-60 second tape of their scene using only sound effects. I found that I had to advise students that there would be silent sections so that they would not fill the tape with a nonstop stream of sounds.

The next step is for each group to record the taped sounds on paper with symbols. They may have to draw swirling lines, heavy dots and objects such as owls and branches. For each group these tapes and pictures serve to stimulate a group dance. When creating the dance, ask your students to respond to the sounds and symbols, represent actions and objects in the tape, and match the length of the sound and symbol recording. Doing this challenges the students, but after all of this work, your students will have given the whole scene a lot of thought. I found that my students discovered their movement sequences very quickly and were eager to share dances with the entire class.

Transforming Nature Art into Dance

In this transformation activity, students learn skills of collaboration and flexibility and develop their awareness of the environment.

Every time students respond to print or sounds with movement, they are bringing something to life. To prepare for this activity, you'll need to arrange the children in groups. Ask each group to create a nature scene backdrop on mural paper. One book that is built upon the theme of bringing objects to life is *The Incredible Painting of Felix Clousseau* by Jon Agee. The children may gather ideas or themes from any factual nature books or fictional tales already in your classroom.

Once the theme is chosen, the students in each group can create a backdrop. One representative from each group can gather supplies: a piece of mural paper, markers and crayons. The details added by each painter can then give rise to movements; each painter explores, creates and memorizes a movement phrase inspired by the backdrop detail.

In my classroom, one group chose to create a waterfall scene. The student who captured the movement of the grass around the edges of the paper wove in, out and around the edge of the space, swaying in the breeze. The child who added the rock kept his shape and remained still while the water dropped from high to low level repeatedly.

Encourage the children to put all of their sections together to create a dance based on and set against the pictured backdrop. Truly transforming!

Extending the Activity: You can expand the activity by doing more movement and adding sound. Encourage your students to return to their original backdrop and include additional details. A second and third series of movements will arise, which in turn can be added to their original dance. Your students' discussion could turn to finding suitable accompaniment for their piece and they may select balances and shapes to hold in tableaux when they are not moving.

Capturing Nature on the Move

This multi-media activity encourages children to explore nature in three dimensions. As students engage in it they will develop their skills in cooperation, analysis, decision making and presentation.

To start this activity you will need pictures of nature, which may include a storm at sea, a starry sky, and a city street. Take these picture images from calendars, post cards or vertical file materials, or select pages from your classroom books.

You'll need to divide the class into small groups of three or four children. Ask each group to select one picture to work from. Their task is to bring the chosen picture to life. Help the children to identify three actions that are happening in the picture, and encourage them to create a movement phrase for each.

I found that I needed to remind students that a movement phrase begins with a starting shape and includes an action and an ending shape. One group of students chose a picture of a volcanic eruption. The three actions that they identified included erupting, oozing, and hardening. All of these actions lent themselves very well to creating a movement phrase.

In order to add some form to their creation, you might ask that each of the three phrases be eight counts long: you can provide accompaniment, beating a regular pattern of eight counts to set the length and create consistency. Also, you might give your students some options for accompaniment; perhaps they can choose from recorded music, rhythm sticks or drums.

This activity proved so successful in my classroom that we ended up sharing it at an assembly, putting the pictures onto slides which were projected onto the stage screen, and having the students move in their phrases in front of the slides. And it all began with a calendar!

Across the Curriculum

• Visual Art: Slide making

Working with blank slides available from photography stores and overhead acetates, students can create designs and scenes based on nature. They might enjoy exploring colours, shapes and textures using different media to create these slides. In turn, the slides can be used to stimulate movement experiences.

In one class I worked with, students used the slides to stimulate movement, devising movement phrases as outlined in Creating a Living Environment. When they viewed the slides, they did the viewing in the gym, and each person that responded to a slide brought the scene to life through movement. A movement variation on the home slide show!

• Music: Creating sound-effect tapes

Students may choose to develop a library of accompaniment tapes. This library could include music that lends itself to dance, describes scenes or evokes an emotion. Beyond tapes already produced for this chapter's activities, students may decide to create more tapes for movement accompaniment.

• Drama: Making a shadow puppet theatre

Shadow puppets are easy to make and can be used to extend the idea of shadow work in the classroom. *The Enchanted Caribou* by Elizabeth Cleaver features shadow puppets for all of the black-and-white illustrations and includes puppet patterns at the back of the book.

You might choose to make a shadow puppet theatre using a black construction paper frame with white tissue paper stretched across the screen area. Students could explore the use of hands as puppets with it. Working with popsicle sticks and black construction paper, they could make their own shadow puppets, then use them to create or retell a puppet story.

Your class can make background sets to accompany many of its drama presentations. Invite the children to use a discarded appliance box and place different scenes on different sides so that they can change the scenes easily.

• Language Arts: Creating a coffee table book

You can make a coffee table book by laminating and spiralbinding the scenic pictures created by the students. This book can later give rise to written stories describing the scene, event or experience. By responding to the pictures, students can capture details and descriptions in their writings.

• Physical Education: Mirroring and following in the gym

Students can dance with their shadows and as they pause in a balance, their partners can outline the shadows with sidewalk chalk on the pavement. They can repeat the activity several times, changing roles and seeing the resulting overlay of images on the ground.

• Reflection: Using an environmental journal

The activities in this chapter have an environmental focus. Invite your students to keep an environmental journal or diary in which they can reflect about nature through picture making, written response and research.

3 Gaining an Understanding of Human Relationships

The structure of the family and community has changed significantly over the last decade. Children are now born into smaller families and generally have fewer opportunities to interact with others. At the same time, they are expected to gain sophisticated social skills. Children can develop their abilities to cooperate while actively participating in school activities. They can learn to collaborate effectively within society as they work and play with other students and adults.

In order for students to play their roles in the community, they must develop a positive sense of self, and respect and the ability to care for others. In the school system, we must provide opportunities for the development of effective interpersonal and decision-making skills. Strong social skills of collaboration and cooperation are necessary in all areas of study, particularly for small- and large-group work. In a society that provides many team situations, our students must be effective team players. We can build a community of learners by providing students with a supportive environment in which they can develop their own abilities and learn with others.

We can teach children how to help one another and how to work effectively with partners and in groups; however, they must be given time to practise cooperative skills. This chapter provides students with many opportunities to interact and to apply these skills. The activities are organized so that students work together to support learning.

Students begin by exploring ways to communicate ideas and information; then they explore roles and responsibilities, trust relationships and group interaction. In each case, the activities relate to books that introduce elements of interpersonal relationships. Through participation in the activities, students can build self-esteem and recognize the strength and importance of relationships.

All books delve into characters and their relationships with other characters to some extent. When selecting a cluster of books for use in this chapter, give attention to those books that highlight cooperative and collaborative efforts. The books that you are featuring in your classroom program should provide a satisfactory basis for exploring interpersonal relationships.

Developing Relationships

Untangling the Web Together

To encourage the children to develop their ability to work together, you can introduce this cooperative game in which children work in a group to solve presented problems. The children will learn about the need to communicate, take turns and compromise.

You might begin by reviewing with the class a book that highlights the interdependence of friends. *The Fight* by Betty D. Boegehold provides a good review of the connection between people. With the class, identify the aspects of the relationship in the book you choose. You may spark a lively discussion about student relationships.

Now, time for the game. Give each of the children a coloured piece of tissue paper, and invite them to join with other children who have the same colour of paper. Instead of joining hands, the children hold onto each other's tissue paper randomly across the group to form a tangled circle. You can challenge them to move as creatively as possible without tearing or letting go of their tissue. Or, you might want to have your students tangle themselves up and then see if they can become untangled. You could invite students to do the following:

- have everyone move at the same time
- move one after the other
- have only one person or two people move
- use low, middle and high levels of movement

I found that I needed to encourage the children to hold the tissues of children they didn't usually interact with; otherwise, they merely joined with a good friend, leaving several members of a group out of the web. The tissue really helped to avoid any hand-holding problems.

Extending the Activity: I found that varying the nature and length of material held between group members led to fun. You might want to introduce scarves, streamers, elastics and cloth.

As the students tried each of the different materials in my classroom, they discovered many new aspects of their games. The elastic, for example, allowed them to move a greater distance apart, which in turn allowed more stretch and strain in their movement. The more colourful objects, such as scarves and streamers, gave the game a maypole dance look, and the woven strands of colours made the interrelations in the group visible.

Lining Up Right

To encourage students to become effective communicators, you might want to let them play this Line-up game. The children will need to talk, listen and act in response to the challenges presented.

Have the children organize themselves into a line according to a specified criterion. For example, challenge them to put their bodies into an orderly line according to month of birth. That means that those born in January will move to the front of the line, while those with birthdays in December will go to the back of the line. The fun starts when there are several children born on the same day!

Information line-ups that you might want to try include:

- height of knees
- physical attributes such as hair or eye colour
- number of buttons on clothing
- length of clothing
- shoe size
- length of hair
- colour tones of clothing

You might want to draw your students' attention to the process involved in the activity by asking questions such as, "Can you do it faster?" or "What are some of the things you can do to get organized faster?"

This activity naturally focuses on comparing people to one

36

another. In order to set the tone, I found it helpful to share *The Story of Ferdinand* by Munro Leaf. Ferdinand the bull sends the timeless message that we are all unique, must make our own decisions, and should respect individual differences. Any story that focuses on personal strengths and discusses the strengths of others will work.

Throughout the activity, students in my classroom could be overheard complimenting one another. Comments such as "Raviv listened to my suggestions" and "we'll try Joan's suggestions and then Michael's" were heard.

The line-ups students created took on interesting formations. For example, students lined up along the side of and in front of or in a body pyramid, with bodies built upon each other.

Throughout this game, I found it helpful to review and apply these rules: keep your hands and feet to yourselves, make space for others and form groups without bothering others.

The Role Game

Having children play a variety of roles helps them develop the communicating skills of listening actively, taking turns and making eye contact.

You can lead into a role game by reading the picture book *Wilfrid Gordon McDonald Partridge* by Mem Fox. This book explores the relationship between a young boy and an aging friend who has lost her memory. So often children are seen as those to be supported and helped; this book sends the message that we can all play a role in nurturing and supporting others.

The game roles and movements are these:

Baby: hands up to be picked up
Child: walking
Parent: hands on hips

A child is faster than a baby, a parent is faster than a child, and a baby is faster than a parent. Students benefit from the practice of these three roles before the game begins.

Divide the children into two groups, one on either side of a line. Each group forms a huddle and quietly selects a character. The children then do each of the character movements, saying "baby," "child," and "parent" as they move. On the fourth movement, they declare their role, saying the name and showing the movement.

A "race" begins. The children chase the babies, the parents chase the children, or the babies chase the parents. A wall represents safety.

As a result of this and other races, the membership of each group changes. Different numbers of students may end up standing on any one line at a time. I found it useful to debrief and discuss the changing roles during the game so that children could gain a better understanding of the roles and responsibilities of family members.

Role Playing with a Partner

Trusting a Friend

You might want to have your students explore qualities of friendship by playing trust games. Such games present a physical challenge that requires both members of a pair to work together to meet the challenge. By playing trust games, children will gain practice in working together to solve problems and make decisions.

You might want to prepare the children for trust games by introducing a book that focuses on trust and friendship. I have found that the book *Willy and Hugh* by Anthony Browne works well. In order to gain partners (or friends), the children can determine which day of the week their birthday will fall on this year. Then, saying the day out loud, students can walk around the room to find a classmate with the same day. That match can then become a pair of "friends."

There are many different trust games that your children can play. You might want to choose from the following.

Human Springs: Students face partners, standing about one foot apart. Both students stretch palms forward and teeter until they meet. They should try pushing back to their original positions then try to increase the distance between each other. How far can each pair go?

Back to Back: Partners sit back to back with elbows joined. On the signal they both stand up without letting go of the arms. Can they travel around the room? Return to sitting?

Beach Ball Balance: Partners share a beach ball without using their hands. Can they find a variety of ways to balance the ball as they move around the room? Can they balance it between their heads? stomachs? or feet? Can they do different movements as they balance the ball?

These activities proved to be very worthwhile in my classroom. After working closely with a partner, we discussed ways to manage differences, and such discussions recurred throughout the school day. We talked about the need for partners to state their position or problem, the need to see the problem from another viewpoint and the methods that they could use for negotiating, mediating, and reaching consensus. Of course, we didn't stop here, but kept working in partners to develop our cooperation skills.

Leading and Following

Students can learn to give and take direction when working in pairs. You might want to introduce this leading and following game to your students. They will learn to follow the directions of others, to lead the actions of others and become more aware of their relationships to others in the process.

To begin the game, you can ask the children to find a partner with the same length of hair. Students then work in pairs: one as a leader and the other as a follower. The leader moves across the floor using a variety of traveling actions. The partner responds by using the same traveling actions. You can encourage students to use different actions and to remain close to their partners and to alternate leader and follower roles.

Students can explore elements of relationships in movement. Ask the children to choose from the following list and move

- near to each other
- far from each other
- away from each other
- meeting each other
- side to side with each other
- facing each other
- shadowing each other

I found that the leader must lead with relatively complex movements while the follower must pay attention to the details of the movements. Students enjoy experimenting with moving in unison and moving consecutively within their roles of leader and follower. In my classroom, the children reacted to the activity by laughing and yelling challenges, daring their partners to follow the movements exactly.

Role Playing and Reacting

To encourage the children to explore the roles that they might take now or later in life, you might want to suggest an action/reaction game. The children will learn about various roles by performing them for their partners, who in turn react to the performance.

You might begin by reviewing with the class a book that highlights various roles. I have found that *The Very Best of Friends* by Margaret Wild works well. With the class, make a list of the roles and responsibilities you find in the book you choose. You can expand this list by generating ideas from the children about their own lives. You may well spark a lively discussion about responsibilities. Help the children to identify their own responsibilities and the importance of these. Your final list might have such headings as these:

- sister
- friend
- teacher

- doctor
- cousin
- brother

Next comes the fun part. To begin the game, ask a child to select a role from the list. Without saying a word, the child should assume the role through actions and movement. Once the other children can identify the role, encourage them to react to it. Ask the children to take partners, so that they can practise role playing with each other. I found that the role of doctor worked well in my classroom. The "doctor" lifted an imaginary mallet to hit the partner's knee. It took a few tries, but soon the partner's legs responded to this reflex check.

Repeat the game several times so that both partners have a chance to play a role and play a reactor.

Extending the Activity: You might want to play this family game in groups of four children. You will need to create sets of family cards, with four names in each family, for example, Father, Mother, Amy and Scott Smith. The cards are mixed up and distributed among the players. The game begins with everyone moving about the room trading cards with other players. At the signal from the leader, all members of each family must find one another and sit down on one chair: Father at the bottom, then Mother, then son and daughter.

After we had tried this in the classroom several times, we decided to add the challenge of silence. As a result, the groups went through some interesting processes in order to find their families.

Working Together as a Group

Trio Triangle

Trio Triangle is a small-group cooperative game in which the group must work together to protect one another. This game includes all students and encourages them to work together equally. In the process, children learn teamwork skills and responsibility and develop some good work habits.

There are many beautiful children's books that deal effectively with the theme of cooperation. One that works well is *Chicken Man* by Michelle Edwards. Whichever story you select, you can engage children in a discussion of the roles and responsibilities in the story and of the interdependence of the characters.

Ask your students to form groups. I have found that by cutting calendar pictures into three pieces, and distributing one piece of the puzzle to each student, students can form groups by finding the matching pieces. Once in a group, children can rotate the roles of observer, encourager and time keeper.

Now that the children are ready, ask them to form a physical triangle with joined hands, and place an object, such as a traffic cone, in the centre. Challenge your students to try to have one member of the triangle touch the cone without anyone in the group dropping hands. As the children pull and push, this game can become a game of strength and body weight.

Change the game by encouraging your students to focus on not touching the cone. This forces them to move out of a competitive spirit into a cooperative one.

Once the students had this great lesson in working interaction, we could explore a little further. Still working with a triangular formation, I challenged my students to create a movement phrase that explored the space between the group members. You can invite your students to create a dance of three movement phrases: one in which group members meet, one in which they part and one in which they move simultaneously. Once again, students showed full phrases, each with a beginning shape, clear traveling action and an ending shape.

The results of this task proved interesting: the students had to work as a group on many levels. First, they brainstormed, then they clarified ideas, elaborated on shared ideas, saw the consequences of their ideas, organized the information and made their solutions.

As your students work together, you'll need to look for sensitive responses to each other's movements and for an awareness of each other.

Forming Circles

Encourage your students to create and present with this small-group, cooperative movement activity. As they participate, children will develop skills in negotiating and reaching agreement, group functioning, processing and creativity.

To begin the activity, ask the children to place themselves in order according to the length of their shoelaces; if their shoes do not have laces, have them consider the length of Velcro fasteners or of shoe tongues. Then, divide the line of students into smaller lines of five or so. Ask each line of children to curve to form a closed circle. You can then invite each circle group to create a circle of shapes. Then, choosing the action of splitting, linking, passing between, or twining, the members of the circle should explore ways of using one action within their formation.

You can have the students explore the next action within a modified formation; a circle that is larger, smaller, overlapping, or elongated. Once again, students participate in problem solving as a group and reaching consensus. You can challenge each group to create an action phrase for each of the two actions chosen.

Extending the Activity: Your students can manipulate the circle formation more fully with this extension activity. Have students begin with fingers touching. Invite them to continue on with the movement phrases created earlier, but this time have the group use actions to expand and contract the circle, losing and regaining touch. Your students may want to modify their earlier movement phrases to include some of their discoveries.

Dancing a Study of Alienation

In my own classroom, I found that the issue of loneliness and alienation emerged frequently in discussions. I also found that books such as *The Story of Ferdinand* helped to bring substance to our discussions on this topic. You may wish to select a book to introduce this topic, or capitalize on class discussion initiated by your students.

Working with your class, develop a list of aspects of human relationships. Encourage students to discuss each aspect listed. Now, challenge your students to create a dance based on one of the identified themes. You might choose to address one of these movement relationships:

- being near to another person
- far from another person
- parting from another
- meeting another
- side to side with a partner
- facing each other
- shadowing one another
- leading and following a partner

You can encourage students to discover many different ways of using the relationship in the group movement. Ask your students to begin by creating one eight-count phrase. One of my groups chose the theme of alienation and the relationship aspect of *near to* for their movement phrase. Working in a closed line, four dancers traveled along the diagonal while the lone dancer tried unsuccessfully to join the line. Be sure to give your students time to select and refine their first movement phrase before continuing on.

Once that original phrase is set, you can challenge students to take that phrase and repeat it, changing the group formation used. By this point, your students will have developed a sixteen-count dance. Those students who are ready to step a little further can create yet another eight-count phrase, varying the original eight-count phrase by changing the direction, size, level, speed, facing direction, effort, shape, or number of people dancing. The product is a fuller, yet connected study of alienation, isolation and loneliness.

Across the Curriculum

• Language Arts: Choral reading

Choral reading is an interesting way to have students interact as they read. It doesn't matter which poem or story is selected, just as long as students explore different interactions in the reading. Although the format may vary, you might choose to try one of the following possibilities:

- Everyone reads at the same time;
- Each person reads one line;
- Two people read one line, two other people read the next;
- Different combinations of people read the different lines.

• Drama: Role playing

This may be done with the support of a dress-up box, or as a development of plot and character within readings and class experiences. Students can select roles and act out the characters in any given story.

• Music: Relationship rap

Students can create a rap about those people around them, in the class, home or community. Encourage them to consider the represented people's names, roles and responsibilities.

• Visual Art: Creating a wall mural

Children can work collaboratively to create a large wall mural. The topic or theme of that mural may evolve from class discussions.

• Media: Television show

Children can create a television show that deals with interrelationships. For the television in my classroom, we used a box with a large square cut out and rolled paper on a paper towel roll to change the scenes. You might challenge your students to explore how what someone does has an impact on someone else.

4 Communicating Through Movement

Students must know how to communicate in order to be a part of society. Through conversation students share experiences and understandings which in turn helps to create a sense of community. They can also use movement as communication, as one kind of talk needed for sharing ideas within the classroom.

Through movement students may see, both in their bodies *and* in their minds, what is being communicated in print. As they engage print with their bodies, children can imagine and visualize the real action: the conflict, aggression and human interaction. They can then communicate through movement, as well as written and spoken language, their feelings and thoughts of the print experience — this depth of experience will lead to a developed sense of appreciation and inquiry about words and movement.

Students should have opportunities to respond as movers to conversations or to respond to movement as writers. In time, conversations through movement can shape how the children articulate what is happening around them. Through the combined exploration of language and movement students participate in the dynamic process of communication necessary in all subject areas.

In order for words and sounds to make sense to a child, they must have some relation to the child's experiences. Movement experiences allow students to expand awareness through the body and form important mind and body connections. In this chapter students will speak words and make sounds through body motion and listen to the messages created by the body in motion. Many of the literature sources used, such as *Listen to the Rain* and *Night Noises*, feature richly descriptive vocabulary and sounds, stimulating interesting movement responses. As students develop the mind and body connection, they can retain more information, find greater enjoyment in reading content, and learn more actively. Communicating through movement—a meaning-making process.

Communicating Moods

Making Physical Introductions

To encourage the children to introduce themselves and learn about others in the classroom, you might want to suggest this icebreaker. The children will learn to clearly state their names, select corresponding movements, and recall and sequence names and movement. This introduction activity is a wonderful way to develop concentration and memory skills in students.

You can begin this activity by introducing your own name through movement. I chose to do this with a stretch and a jump (J-a-n et). Your students will probably be surprised by your actions and will eagerly want to introduce themselves. I found that this activity helped me considerably when I did not know a particular group of children well and they were anxious that I know their names!

Help the students by discussing the syllabic nature of words. Draw their attention to the syllables in their own names, then invite them to discover movements to convey their names. As it turns out, the syllabic length and nature of children's names are often captured in their movements.

I found that aspects of the children's personalities came through clearly. Julian, a young fellow bursting with energy, introduced himself with three punctuated, gravity-defying leaps. Drew's one movement took him droopily to the floor. André, sensing the sound and flow of his name, introduced himself through two slow and sustained stretches, very languid and sinewy.

This activity succeeds well with older students if they work in a circle. One after another, the children can introduce themselves by saying and moving to their name. You might choose an even more challenging approach by asking the children to do the preceding activity, adding their names and movements to those already given. This forces them to recall names and movements. You can watch the laughter as the last few members of the circle jaggedly move and speak along.

Extending the Activity: You can challenge the children to choose movements that reflect their personalities, interests and hobbies. Begin by asking your students to turn to a friend and teach that friend their name and movement. Once ready, children can join the two names and movements together to form a movement sequence.

The obvious contrasts in movements can be quite surprising. I found that the movements chosen were very telling about the personalities and interests of the students. One student commented, "Now you know I do karate," after delivering a punchy name.

Responding to the Mood of Music

Students listen to and recognize the rhythm, pattern, pitch and tempo of music, developing their sensitivity to the emotion of music and their aesthetic awareness.

To introduce this activity, select a piece of music that explores a variety of feelings. Music that features nature sounds or a range of emotions, with changes in tempo and tone within one track, work well. One such recording is *Movin'* by Hap Palmer. After asking the children to remain still during silence, play the music and ask the children to capture the mood of the music in their movement.

You will probably want to begin with frequent short sessions of music and gradually lengthen the time in between stops. You might challenge the children to reflect the emotion in their movements. Each piece of music will elicit different types of movements, ranging from smooth glides and balances to jagged punches and kicks.

Extending the Activity: You can present these challenges to students:

• imitating the rhythm of the music;
• moving in opposition to the music;
• moving with the music as a general background sound, but responding only to the mood created.

As a result of this learning experience, students will develop sensitivity and responsiveness to music.

Physically Moving Words

In this descriptive word activity, students locate and select descriptive words. As they do so, they develop their processing skills, listening to and interpreting words and creating a mental image of those words.

You'll need to begin with a book that is rich in descriptive words. Two books that I have found to be successful are *Faint Frogs Feeling Feverish and Other Tantalizing Tongue Twisters* and *The Headless Horseman Rides Tonight*. After reading through the book that you have chosen, revisit sections of your text and ask your students to listen for their favourite phrases. Each student can then record one descriptive phrase on a post-it, then put the post-it on the board to create a list of descriptive words. The list that we created in my classroom included these phrases:

- busily building
- driving dangerously
- eagerly eating
- painting portraits
- soulfully sighing...

Invite the children to stand still in a start position. Slowly read the first phrase on the list. As each word is read, students respond with movement. They can do so slowly so that they can move smoothly from one word and phrase to the next.

I found that the following interesting pattern emerged. At first, the children responded with one action of short length. As they relaxed, the children's actions lengthened, almost matching the syllables in the word. I learned that I needed to watch the cadence and melody of my reading as these affected the nature of the students' movement responses. In some cases, children moved in the role of a character, focusing on the object rather than the descriptive word and how that felt. At other times, students moved to explore the descriptive word.

Afterwards, I invited each child to draw a picture to capture the feeling of one of the words and add that to the board as well. The pictures captured the different approaches to the movements, with some focused on feelings and others focused on objects being explored.

You may want to invite the children to consider the words that they moved through and select the strongest movement. Ask them to refine that movement and present it to a friend. Can the friend identify the word that gave rise to the movement phrase?

Interpreting Sounds with a Partner

Creating Movements That Lead to Sounds

In this listening and responding activity students focus on sounds. Children create a movement and sound phrase with the structure of a movement phrase. As your students become involved, they will develop skills in analyzing and evaluating sounds, as well as environmental awareness.

You'll need to begin by selecting a source of sounds. One that I have found works well is *The Little Old Lady Who Was Not Afraid of Anything* by Linda Williams. You can ask the children to accompany the text with their own sounds as you read through the book. The stimuli identified in your text might include:

- clomp, clomp
- wiggle, wiggle
- shake, shake
- clap, clap
- nod, nod
- boo, boo

You may find that many of your students also respond to the sounds with movements that capture the feeling of the word. For example, *wiggle wiggle* may generate a swishy swashy sound and movement, while *clomp clomp* could lead to forceful contact with a surface, creating a stomping sound. You might choose to discuss other sounds that can be made with the voice, such as moaning, cackling, giggling, grunting, honking, sniffing, roaring, gasping, snickering, murmuring, hissing, and clicking. Invite your students to form their own two-word connections. Among those that we discovered were these:

- screeching chalk
- eyes moving
- heart pounding
- clock ticking
- foot stomping
- finger snapping

Now the fun begins! Ask students to work with partners to discover movements that give rise to the sound. They can begin with a favourite description and explore it through movement. For clocks ticking, students might use a swing and pendular movement which travels sideways across a smaller and smaller distance, capturing the word through movement. You can challenge children to use the movement to expand the sound. My students decided that *screeching chalk* was a series of jagged body movements, full of angles and sharp changes in direction. The movement lasted only as long as the accompanying screech.

Making Sounds in Movement

By making body responses to sounds, students develop skills in decision making, sequencing, analysis and evaluation in this interpretation activity.

To prepare students, select something that is rich in sound, perhaps a sound recording, environmental sounds, music or a picture book. I found that *Night Noises* by Mem Fox works well. Working with the children, create a list of sounds from the chosen source. Your list may contain some of the following sounds:

- click, clack
- crunch, crunch
- murmur, mutter, shhh
- knick, knack, knock

Challenge the children to create a movement phrase for the first several words on your list. Ask each pair to select a favourite word and develop a movement phrase with a beginning shape, traveling action and an ending shape. Students can repeat the process for two other words so that three movement phrases are created.

The real fun begins as students create a second list of potential noises. Other words that my children recalled included knock, yell, knick, snick, and catcher. The noises included *whoo*, *thunder*, *bark bark*, *woof woof*, *click click*, *shhhh* and *ouch*. *Whoo* was interpreted as a long, extended movement performed simultaneously by two partners, while *ouch* was a series of quick, large whole-body recoils (noisy too!).

The students will need to decide on the order of the events. Can the remainder of the class identify the words in order?

Expressing Phrases Physically

You might choose to introduce this listening game to your students to capture the feeling of words in movement. Participation in this activity will lead students to synthesize, process, conclude and produce movement to convey information.

For this activity, you'll need to select a source of imagery. I found that the book *Listen to the Rain* by Bill Martin, Jr., and John Archambault works well. As you read the story, invite students to listen for the sentence or phrase that conjures the clearest image in their minds. Students can then record their chosen phrases on pieces of paper with their partners. You can encourage children to recall and combine words in different orders to create distinct meanings. Once all students have completed this task, have them deposit all of their papers into a box. The following list serves as a sample of the phrases that my students identified:

- Boom! Crashing, splash, singing
- Sprinkle, tinkle, splashing, singing
- Lightning crash, thunder roar
- Boom! Whisper, whisper, slap
- The whisper, whisper, sing song of rain

The real fun begins as each pair of students selects one piece of paper from the box. Challenge students to create a movement phrase to express the feeling of the phrase on the selected paper. At first, your students may be tempted to respond to the phrases or sentences they selected originally. However, after some exploration time, you'll see interesting images emerge. In my classroom, the soft, repetitive movements (such as sprinkle and tinkle) tended to be done with both partners moving at the same time, using small and quick movements. The loud sounds of rain, such as thunder and *boom*, were captured predominantly with large upward actions, such as jumps and leaps, with limbs jutting jaggedly into the space around. You can even invite partners to join with other pairs to put their movement phrases together to form a richly descriptive dance.

Extending the Activity: Students can continue this activity by sequencing the phrases. Ask students, working as a class, to put the recorded descriptive phrases in order. The sequenced pieces can then be attached to chart paper. Now, partners can respond with their movement phrase as you read their sentence. Once students are finished moving, they may want to write in their journals about this word and movement experience.

Presenting a Movement Suite

Inspired by Action Words

In this sound activity, students work with elements of movement to create a movement suite. In the process, they will analyze and synthesize movement to communicate words and sounds.

To begin the activity, have students work in groups to select an action word or sound from those lists already created in class. Ask students to create an eight-count movement phrase about the selected word or sound. Once the phrase has been completed, encourage groups to repeat it several times to memorize the sequence. They can create a movement suite by taking the original eight counts and creating a separate eight counts by changing one aspect of the movement phrase, such as direction, level, or size.

As they change the original movement phrase, students should create another eight-count phrase. This process is then repeated, again changing another aspect of the original phrase until four eight-count phrases have been created.

In my classroom, one group began with the word *ooze*. Their original movement sequence showed the group in a circle formation on the low level. For the first eight counts they slowly spread the circle wider, lifting and lowering their torsos slightly as they crept sideways. In their second phrase they changed the size of the movement into a wide-ranging sideways traveling action, extending into reaching arms and legs. For the third phrase the group changed the level of their work to the high and middle, keeping the movement the same. For the final eight counts, the group moved alternately away from and toward the group circle, changing the effect from a peeping, oozing movement to a percolating and bubbling movement. The end result was a movement suite of 32 counts.

You'll find that students will need to revisit their created phrases frequently so that they do not forget their sequences.

Extending the Activity: You can have students explore extremes and contrasts in motion within their movement sequences, such as:

- over- and under-statements,
- exaggerated contrasts — large/small, high/low, loud/soft, and
- contradictory voice sounds and movements.

Across the Curriculum

• Media/Music: Creating sound stimulus

Sound-effect tapes can be created by taping in the classroom or school environment. Once you have a collection of sound-effect tapes you can use them as stimuli for writing stories or storytelling, as sound effects for drama or as stimuli for even more movement and dance.

• Visual Art: Breathing life into puppets

Students enjoy creating puppets of all kinds and styles. Of the many kinds, you might want to consider making paper bag, rod or stick puppets, shadow or glove puppets or even marionettes. There are many books that outline the procedure for making puppets, but you might want to begin with simple sock puppets. Students can glue buttons and yarn onto a sock, and can even add clothes. Of course, the puppets can then be used to revisit many of the stories introduced in this chapter, capturing some of the movement and feelings experienced in the process.

• Music/Art: Responding to the mood and atmosphere of music

Many sound recordings are available to schools. You can play a recording as students work on visual art and challenge them to capture some aspect of the recording, such as mood or rhythm, in classroom picture and print making.

• Language Arts: Word lists, banks, and responses

This chapter is full of activities that arise from the exploration of words. Many of them give rise to word list creation, and these lists in turn can be used to support class writing and reading programs.

5 Communicating Poetry Through Body Talk

Body language plays an important role in effective communication. Our body stance, posture and movements communicate information about us. Through body language we express and communicate personal experiences and feelings.

In this chapter, we'll take a closer look at body talk. By doing so, we can become more aware of the messages we are sending and more receptive to the messages sent from others. As we recognize and respond to our non-verbal language and that of others, we create a more responsive community of communicators.

We can use our bodies to understand and communicate information deliberately. The body is an excellent vehicle for experiencing thoughts, ideas and events and for conveying the resulting emotional experience to self and others. The physical experience of body language lends reality to a learning experience, bringing thoughts and emotions into the concrete sphere of body experience.

Activities in this chapter will allow students to enjoy the kinesthetic experiences of poetry through body actions. Students will respond to mood, telling tales through body movements, sending messages physically and creating group tableaux. Opportunities to use the body to send and receive information include visualization, interpretation, and mastery of gestures and body movements. Narration is introduced to support communication of poetry.

Responding to Rhythm

Catching the Body Part Beat

Students use non-verbal communication to convey emotions. As they participate in this activity, they develop their aesthetic awareness of rhythm and tempo.

You'll need to begin with a poetry selection that features a good, contagious beat and refers to parts of the body. One collection of poetry suitable at the early primary level is *Stamp Your Feet* by Sarah Hayes. I chose poems from Michael Rosen's *Freckly Feet and Itchy Knees* because of the catchy rhythm and the direct references to moving body parts.

As you read through your selection, you can invite your students to wiggle and jiggle, sway and tap body parts to the rhythm of the poem. Once you have read through it a few times, you can work with your class to identify emotions. Your list may include anger, happiness, sadness and surprise.

Now, you can revisit your chosen poem, reading with different tones of voice. As you read angrily, happily and sadly, invite students to respond. You might be surprised by how the emotions change your students' movements. I found that "bellies" was the most fun. I watched students roll, stretch and collapse as they tried to move their bellies to my full-of-surprise reading. The slightly off kilter humour created by the combination of moving body parts and emotions will lead your students to explore some wacky body part dances!

Extending the Activity: You can also introduce your students to other body part dances. Consider creating a knee dance, feet dance, or hand and shoulder dance as a whole class! My class had such a wonderful time that they even wrote their own dance poem:

> feet that are running,
> jogging, walking,
> feet that are jumping,
> jogging, skipping.
>
> hands that are clapping,
> shaking, wobbling,
> jiggling, moving,
> cutting, ripping hands.

shoulders that wiggle
round, up and down,
back and forth,
round and round.

Feeling Poetry

Children can respond to poetry with movement in this activity. As they do so, they will develop receiving, processing and communicating skills.

There are many excellent poetry collections. I chose to use *Rhymes Around the Day* and *The Headless Horseman Rides Tonight*. You might begin with students sitting or standing on the floor. Read your chosen poem and invite all students to respond with movement. The first time through the poem, you could find that the children respond with small, careful movements, such as fingers drumming or tapping. You can discuss the feeling and the atmosphere created in each poem. Your discussion might cover such questions as:

- How does the poem feel? Is it heavy or light?
- What is the tempo of the poem? Is there a regular beat?
- Does the tempo of the poem change? Is it fast or slow?
- What did you think of as you heard the poem? Did you create a picture in your mind?

The discussion should inspire students to look a little deeper into the poem and to respond to its detail. I found that as a result of the discussion, the movement responses changed from finger drumming to total body drumming, alternating with small body-part movements. Many of my students alternated the weight of their movements, switching from firm stamps to light taps.

I found that I had to bring more attention to the reading of the poetry in order to capture different feelings and moods. Choosing distinctive poems was helpful. The distinction helped the children to capture the feeling in their movements. Clearly, movement made any emotion much more concrete. Students often find it much easier to talk about their movement experience than to discuss the atmosphere or mood of a poem.

Extending the Activity: You might want to extend the poetry response activity by exploring the following variables:

- students respond to every other line, otherwise freeze in a shape;

- students respond for an entire stanza, otherwise remain still;
- students move as they wish, when they wish;
- students accent movements by placing a large or heavy movement at the end, middle or beginning of a line or phrase.

My students enjoyed the ownership and the different challenges that each variable presented to them. Their movements captured a far wider range of mood and atmosphere, highlighting, and in some cases creating, new feeling for the poetry.

Sharing Body Talk

Reading Body Messages

Students can explore a variety of body shapes in this poetry response activity. As they work to represent the poetry, students develop skills in interpretation, presentation and communication.

To begin this activity you'll need some active poems. I chose to use "Hello, sir," "Miss Polly" and "What do you suppose" from *Zoomerang a Boomerang* by Caroline Parry. Once you have read through the selected poems, you can ask the children to pick a favourite section from one of them. Children should make frozen shapes to capture their chosen section. Once they are all ready with their frozen shapes, encourage them to show their partners the shapes. Then, they can challenge their partners to identify the part of that poem they are representing. In some cases, students will choose body shapes to represent the main idea of the poem; in other cases they will capture one small character or section of the poem.

Initially, we found that the partners could easily find the message in the body and identify the poem. But as we changed over and the second partner presented, the shapes became a little more obscure. It became increasingly difficult to read the message in the body!

Extending the Activity: After each partner presents, the watcher can ask the mover questions about the poem fragment captured. The mover should answer only with movement, adding details to the shape and clarifying the movement message.

Extending Poetry and Movement

Children can listen to, identify and elaborate upon the thoughts of others in this activity. The life skills that they will develop include processing information and communicating effectively with others.

Choose a poetry selection that has clear imagery and illustrations with large, clearly defined shapes. We found that the poem "Sliding" from *All Join In* by Quentin Blake works well. Before beginning, ask students to get partners and select a working space in the room. As you read the poem, children should take a shape to depict something from the poem. Their partner then takes the shape and changes it in some way, making it bigger, smaller, thinner, whatever.

One pair in my room explored a knee bend. The knee bend was in turn expanded with the partner placing feet wider apart and dropping the weight lower. The knee bend began as a blip of a movement and settled into a slow, solemn lowering. Another movement, a slide along the floor, began as a stretched step, which was in turn expanded into a long-reaching and stretched slide.

You can invite students to switch roles several times, changing an aspect of the movement with each transition. Some of the changes made by students might include making the movement suddenly, stretching it over a longer time period, making it firmly on the ground, or lightly touching the ground.

In each case, you can focus on how the movement has transformed. In some cases, students can recall different movements that they modified together. At first, students selected feet and arm movements. Over time, they involved more of their bodies in creating changes. This activity serves as a great method for gathering snippets of original movement.

Extending the Activity: You could have one person introduce a movement while the partner adds word descriptions to that movement. What started as a *swish* (an undulating movement back and forth with the arms) can evolve into a whole body pendulum swing, or a *swish swash smoothly*. Other descriptive word combinations that the children might identify include

- pounding hopping
- quickly clapping
- jumping strongly

This will lead you into a whole new exploration which may result in your own class poetry collection, developed through partnerships among students.

Interpreting Poetry in a Group

Pass the Poem Around the Circle

A feeling from a poem is captured by one student in movement, and then passed all around a circle. Receiving skills, such as listening for a purpose, exploring information sources, analyzing and processing the communicated information, are developed throughout the activity.

Start with a selected poem, such as "Dawn" from *I Am Phoenix: Poems for Two Voices* by Paul Fleischman. Have the class stand in a circle connected by hands and identify a "starter" and a direction for the message to be sent. Clockwise is the most straightforward. Working line by line, have the students pass their movement response around the circle. I modeled a number of sudden changes of direction for the line "flit." Once I began, the person to my right repeated my movements and the movements were passed around the circle. What interested me was the degree of individuality each member brought to their movements, the timidness of some contrasting with the exuberance of others.

While working with young children, I found it helpful to begin with all seated and using small movements of the head, hands and eyes. These students had difficulty recalling the movements and thinking in advance of their turn. We worked on being prepared and letting movement flow from one person to the next. Ultimately, this activity became a wonderful exercise in communication as students attentively watched the passage of movement. We tried the game in different formations, but found a small, close circle the most effective.

Extending the Activity: You can build on any poem to create a movement sequence. As you follow the lines of the poem, you can send a movement for each line around the circle. Taken as a whole, the poem could give rise to a Circle Dance (or Line Dance, depending on the formation used).

Creating Jigsaw Tableaux

A cooperative learning technique is used in this activity to encourage group members to contribute to a group product. Children will learn to integrate ideas, acknowledge the worth of others and express nonverbal support as they communicate their movement response.

In groups of three, children should select a poem that they

enjoy. We used selections from Jack Prelutsky's *The Headless Horseman Rides Tonight* and "Jump or Jiggle" from *Worms Wiggle, Bugs Jiggle*. Once each group has selected a poem, ask them to select one stanza from within that poem. Each child can then take one line from the chosen stanza to represent with a frozen shape, or tableau. Ask students to add their tableaux together within their groups to create a jigsaw tableau for their stanza. Once each group is ready, you might want to select a narrator to read the whole poem, accompanied by the jigsaw movement of a group during each stanza. The poem will start with one person moving and end with the whole class having moved.

One of my groups chose to work with the poem "The Kraken" from *The Headless Horseman Rides Tonight*. The chosen stanza told of the rise to the surface of an enormous octopus, of the noise created, the vessels caught and squeezed. One student captured the upward grasping of the octopus in a shape, the next represented the vessels floating on the surface with a long, flat and apparently supported shape, and the third chose to suggest the squeeze by bending the body in half, as for a snapping close. Once they were ready with their tableau, we asked an assigned reader to read "The Kraken" out loud. Each student then added his or her tableau during the appropriate section of the stanza, fitting all of the tableau pieces together. "The Kraken" was only one of several poems that we used.

Extending the Activity: The children may be quite eager to try creating their own lines after working with a poem. After working with "Jump or Jiggle," we explored the following word combinations: worms wiggle, fish swish, moons shine, and shoes tap.

After we had an opportunity to explore these words, we chose one combination to expand. Working from Shoes Tap, the children brainstormed the following shoe activities:

> Shoes tap
> Shoes skip
> Shoes jump
> Shoes hop
> Shoes walk
> Shoes stop

As you can well imagine, children can have a lot of fun creating movement tableaux for a poem.

Working with Narrated Poetry

In this activity, students become involved with a narrator as they role play the storyline. They work in small groups to respond with movement to the spoken poetry.

Have student groups choose a poem and a narrator. "What They Said" from *Zoomerang a Boomerang*, as well as poems from *Joyful Noise*, are effective for this activity. Before you begin, explain the role of narrator and ask each group to select at least one child to take the role of the narrator, reading the poem as the rest of the group presents the story in movement.

Invite students to move freely to the accompaniment of the poem. In order to bring structure to this activity, I found that I needed to remind the students to incorporate a start position, actions and clear ending position into their response. Since the poems are short and children have limited opportunity to respond, you might ask the narrator to repeat the reading several times. Encourage the children to find different movements to tell the story each time. The narrator sets the tone and determines the range of emotion presented by students, so that person must be sure to read with expression.

Extending the Activity: The children may want to formalize their final discovery and apply what they have learned back into the poetry. After exploring all of the lines in the poem, each student can select one line and develop a movement phrase for it. At the next narrated poetry reading, students can move with their movement phrase to their selected and prepared line. You might want to open up the activity so that students can respond with their movement phrase to the poetry whenever they want. A beautiful movement mosaic could result.

Studying Expressive Poetry

This activity focuses on emotions within poetry. Prior to beginning, you should select a poem full of strong emotions. "The Spectre on the Moor" from *The Headless Horseman Rides Tonight* carries a strong intangible fear, while "Welcome" from *Scary Poems for Rotten Kids* is full of suggestion and foreboding. Working in groups, students identify and select an emotional state that the poem suggests. In clusters, each group considers the factors or components of that emotional state. For "The Spectre on the Moor" my students elected to focus on the silence, twilight tour, deadly purpose and deadly grasp.

Ignoring the poem, students work to create action phrases based on the components chosen. For my sample group, improvisation included sudden pauses for silence and frequent changes of direction as if to prevent any following. For *deadly purpose* and *deadly grasp*, my students used large, sharp, threatening movements, indicating grasp through continual opening and closing of limbs and people.

Once students have had an opportunity to improvise, ask them to select and refine a movement study on their chosen emotional state, a study of about sixteen to eighteen counts in length. Some may choose to use the reading of the poem to accompany their section, while others will move without any accompaniment at all.

Creating Narrative Dances

Students follow a storyline to select, order, organize and present a Fairy Tale Dance. You may find that this activity works best for Grade 4 and up. Those who participate in it will develop their skills to listen, interpret, sequence, and produce information.

Select a favourite folk or fairy tale rhyme. I chose "Snow White and the Seven Dwarfs" from *Revolting Rhymes*, although many other rhymes would have worked equally well. I found that *Revolting Rhymes* lends itself very well to narrative work, as the storyline can be clearly read by the narrator. Once you have chosen the rhyme, ask students to work in a whole-class group to accompany it with a narrative dance.

We chose to use choral reading and a number of narrators for our dance form, but your class might choose to speak the story or poem out loud, tape the story and only read some words, or alternate a narrator with sound effects. Read through the rhyme several times and divide the rhyme up among the narrators. Once in their groups, the narrators read as the movers identify and formalize two movement phrases for their section. Some children will move to capture the mood of the scene while others will use body shapes and traveling actions to portray their character in movement. Invite narrators to read through their section many times to allow movers to practise their movement sequences. The resulting dance can be presented to the narrative accompaniment of the chosen fairy tale rhyme.

Extending the Activity: You can delve a little deeper into narrative dance creation by expanding the movement motifs of the movers' phrases. Once children have performed the completed dance several times, you can ask them to make a change to their movement sequence. You might want to provide your groups with the following challenges:

- making their phrases faster or slower, or alternating the two
- changing their dances so that they use both heavy and light movements
- making movements larger to fill the space, or smaller and closer to the body
- considering whether their dances should be repeated or removed

These are just some of the possibilities. The students will benefit from the changes. Paying greater attention to detail and refining their movements should make the whole dance more detailed and interesting.

Across the Curriculum

• Language Arts: Chanting poems

Children can create chants to capture the movement sequences evolving out of this chapter's activities. You might choose to have them explore grouping and different combinations of shared and choral reading.

• Media: Creating images with pictures

You can make classroom displays with Polaroid pictures, line drawings or sketches of the poetry tableaux that your class has created. Captions, comments and reflections can be written around, above, below or behind the pictures, recording the whole experience more effectively.

• Music: Relieving tension through music

Students really enjoy moving to music. The more exposure they have to responding to music, the more genuine and expressive their movements become. You might want to put music on as students work and throughout the day. Responding through movement to music can provide students with a welcome release of tension and stress.

• Visual Arts: Making montages

As a response to movement and literature, students can gather magazine pictures and postcards that show emotion. They can then combine the pictures on paper to form montages. Seeing the range of emotions that students capture in their montages may prove interesting. Some students may even choose to create a multi-emotion montage.

6 Discovering and Investigating Rhythm

Our lives are filled with rhythm. We feel it as we breathe, as our heart beats, as we walk, skip and run. Students experience rhythm and repetition daily, too. They drum a rhythm with their fingers, hop on a hopscotch and run around the track. Rhythmic and repetitious movement activities allow children to develop body coordination, awareness and an increased ability to sense the beat and rhythm of their experiences.

Children become aware of rhythmical patterns within their own bodies before the patterns become meaningful and real. Most music programs recognize this need for physical awareness of music and include movement. Kinetic experiences link music concepts with physical sensation to clarify relationships between musical ideas. By exploring walking, leaping and galloping students come to know about changes in tempo and rhythm, first knowing in their bodies and then in their minds.

Activities in this chapter encourage students to investigate tempos, durations, pitches and rhythms. By including these in your classroom, you can support your students in developing a working knowledge and vocabulary of musical and movement concepts.

This chapter focuses on rhythm. The children will have an opportunity to practise, dance, observe and discuss rhythms and patterns. They will start with their own body rhythms and rhythmic responses. They will have a chance to note and capture the rhythm of others through movement patterns, accompanying a partner and following the leader. Throughout the activities, students will create simple movement sequences combining basic traveling actions. They will also use different musical forms in their creations, including canon and AB form. Movement — a wonderful way to make music visible!

Repeating Body Movements

Bopping to Contagious Chants

This activity engages students in rhythmic chanting and movement. As they work to create their own chant and Chant Dance, students will develop music skills of rhythm and tempo, and cooperative skills, such as listening, negotiating, integrating ideas, and staying on task.

For this activity, select a book that features a chant. *The Bop* by Irene Hunt contains a chant that is so contagious that children have trouble sitting still. Read the chosen chant and invite children to move as they listen to the words. You can reread the chant and challenge students to move a specific body part to the rhythm of the chant, or use a different movement each time they move. The children will stomp their feet, clap their hands, snap fingers and wriggle on the floor.

You might want to invite students to accompany the chant with planned movement. You can do this by revisiting the chant and discussing its length. Then, ask students to clap the rhythmic pattern and tap the syllables in each line. Once students are clear about the pattern of the whole chant, they are ready to begin planning their movement.

Many will choose from the movements that they have automatically responded with. You might want to help them by requesting that their movements involve one or two body parts. Have them practise their movements within the chant pattern.

Now they are ready to begin writing. Students can work on their own or with friends to write their own body part bop, keeping the original pattern but changing the words. Throughout the writing process, they may need to keep moving to make certain that their new bop chant will fit their developed bop movement.

Extending the Activity: After choosing a body part, you can ask the children to move that body part when they feel "moved" and stay still otherwise. Doing this means that during the reading of the chant, children will suddenly come to life in waves of movement. You might choose to let the exploration take the movement impulse into different parts of the body: combining two body parts at once, eventually leading into traveling actions around the room.

Responding Rhythmically

This activity provides an exercise in movement control and in response to rhythmic pattern. The children will learn to analyze and discover rhythmic pattern and use rhythm to convey ideas.

You might begin this activity by reviewing with the class a familiar skipping rhyme. I have found that "Cinderella Dressed in Blue" from *Anna Banana* works well. Whatever rhyme you choose, post it on chart paper for easy reference. Select four movements that can be repeated and create a dance by repeating those four movements to the rhythm of the poem. I started with clapping hands, tapping the floor, shaking hands and stomping feet. Then I created a dance by clapping hands during the first line, tapping the floor during the second, shaking hands on the third and stomping feet during the fourth line. Once you have demonstrated the actions, ask the children to follow your lead.

I had to repeat the movements several times so that the students understood the rhythmic pattern clearly. What begins as a teacher-directed activity can quickly develop into a wonderful refocusing and calming activity which the children will want to lead themselves. All of my students wanted to take turns developing a sequence of four repeated movements and leading the class through a patterned dance. They led us through a pattern of four of the following movements:

- swinging
- twisting
- jumping
- tapping
- nodding
- hopping

Extending the Activity: You can challenge students to explore the possible range of a movement and then to repeat the movement working from small to large and large to small. Working with the first four movements listed above, the children can start with a small swing, increase to a large swing and then return to a small.

You might also incorporate changes in direction into your rhythmic responses. Ask the children to move in a different direction for each pair of lines, traveling forward, backward, sideways and on the diagonal. Another change that you can explore is changing the actual rhythmic pattern. Once the children have played with the pattern extensively, they can change the tempo of the pattern, making it faster or slower. At first, the changes may surprise the children, but they will challenge them to keep up.

Pairing Up for Rhythmic Patterns

Leading and Following Actions

You can encourage children to explore partner relationships, through this leader and follower game. Students will set rhythmic actions to a rhyme, learning listening, analyzing, and selection skills.

Basic everyday gestures can be used to start this activity. Or, you might choose a traditional action game. I used the hand waving game from *Street Rhymes Around the World*.

Invite students to identify a gesture to be used, perhaps stamping, clapping, nodding, bowing or waving. Then, ask students to find partners, and identify the leader and the follower within each group. The leader begins by leading with the chosen gesture; the follower imitates the action. Have the children repeat with changed roles.

I encouraged the children to use different actions each time they led their partner. They tried leading with different body parts, changing the rhyme from a hand-waving game to a body-moving game. The natural extensions were shoulders, hands, head and feet; all moved to the rhythm of the rhyme. Eventually, this activity evolved into a game that we played in the gym class to warm up and begin moving.

Once the children have explored a variety of movements, you can challenge them to follow the leader in canon. Repeating a phrase after the leader has just done it may seem easy, but I found that the children were often so eager to follow that they lost the rhythm by not pausing before following.

Making Movement Patterns

Students working with partners will develop their own movement patterns based on sequence, ordering and repetition of movement. As they engage in this activity, they will learn processing skills, and social and group dynamics.

Invite children to work with partners to explore movements on the spot and traveling through space. Ask your students to repeat each movement four times. I found that partners followed each other's lead well as they shared ideas and movements.

You might invite the children to identify four strong movements and repeat each movement four times. When we did this activity, one pair created a pattern of four twists, four jumps, four stretches and four skips. Then have students repeat the four movements, four times in a sequence.

The children will quickly discover a need to choose their actions carefully. Those who choose high-level activities will soon become out of breath. They will need to change their actions to simple movements that they can repeat quickly. When we watched all of the created sequences, the children remarked on the interesting actions and the pattern created by movement and stillness.

Extending the Activity: Some of the children may want to remember their sequences and you may wish to use the sequences in the classroom and in the gym for some physical activity during the day. Ask the children to record their sequences on chart paper. Others might choose some music to accompany their sequence. The music, along with the chart-paper directions, can be used for five-minute fit breaks in your classroom.

You might introduce the children to the challenge of changing time patterns. Children can speed up and slow down their movement sequences: what starts as a high-level sequence with kicks, leaps and fast arm circles might become a series of stretches, large steps and arm sways. Children might also raise and expand and then lower and reduce the sequenced movements gradually, working with the musical terms *crescendo* and *diminuendo*. The children will feel the changes to the quality of their movements.

Beating an Accompaniment to Movement

Let students work with rhythm instruments and body sounds. As they do so, they will develop receiving, listening, interpreting and performing skills.

Have students select a partner to work with. Then, provide each student with a lummi stick. Once the children have explored the sound of the sticks, they should decide which partner will move and which will use the lummi sticks. Now they are ready to accompany an action rhyme. Traditional games serve as good rhyme sources; *Oranges and Lemons* is also a good source of action rhymes.

Read aloud the chosen rhyme and challenge one partner in each pair to move in rhythm, while the other beats the rhythm on the lummi sticks. In one pair in my room, the mover used a twirling movement as the other partner beat the fast rhythm on the floor with the sticks. Have all students switch roles several times. Encourage movers to create greatly varying movements in response to the changing rhythms. Eventually, you might wish to have the children discard the sticks and keep the rhythm with different body parts. Hand clapping and leg slapping are two ways of doing this.

Extending the Activity: You may find that the children are ready to create and respond to their own independent rhythms. You can give the instrumentalists the job of creating their own rhythmic patterns while challenging the "travelers" to respond with movement. Doing this may lead to the creation of short dances with structured rhythmic accompaniment and movement.

We went beyond the use of body sounds and lummi sticks for our rhythmic accompaniment. My students made their own simple noisemakers, such as drums, whistles, cardboard flutes and shakers. Then we explored sound and stillness in the classroom. Each student was asked to remain still whenever their partner's instrument was silent, but to move to the pattern of the instrument when played. The children enjoyed creating and playing a rhythm on the instrument and seeing what movements their partners used to return the rhythm.

Experiencing Musical Forms

Sending Movement in a Round

Children can experience the form of a round as they create movement sequences. As they do so, they will develop non-verbal communication, receiving and interpreting skills.

This game begins with a simple movement pattern being sent in a round to all classmates. You will need to identify a first sender who must prepare a sequence of three repeated movements and pass the sequence to another person. A hop, skip and jump was sent from person to person in my classroom, as if a bee sting was sent around the class.

This activity began in my classroom by accident. We were messing about with sounds when one child repeated a pattern of three movements, three head taps. Three head taps were sent around the room. The next offered three cheek pats, and the final one suggested three foot stamps. I modeled another pattern of three: three head pats, three elbow taps and three hand drummings. This combination was also sent around the room.

The real challenge began when we sent one sequence around the room, immediately followed by a different sequence; as soon as each student completed a sequence, yet another sequence was sent through the room. Truly a round of movement!

The more movement sequences the children create, the more complex and difficult the sequences become to repeat in a round. You can ask your students to change the number of beats, accenting beats, or the speed of the beats.

The activity leads naturally into a matching (echo) game in which the leader leads the group with a movement pattern and the rest of the students echo that pattern. You might choose to use this as a classroom game to focus the students and to fill in the occasional free moments of the day. You can link the sequences all together and try them. Then you might take turns creating and leading patterns.

Comparing the movement pattern at the beginning of the round with what is performed by the last mover interested me. We tried passing the movement after a few counts and found that to be very difficult but not impossible. As the students become skilled, you can have them pass the movement after two or three movements. Recalling and performing the original movement sequence becomes increasingly difficult.

Identifying the Rhythm Pattern Leader

To encourage the children to observe with focus and take risks, you can introduce a guessing game. This whole-group game supports students in taking turns and staying on task as they learn to observe, locate, and identify movement sources. It can fill small time slots in the classroom.

To begin, ask all students to sit in a circle. Then, send one child from the group out of listening distance and select one member of the group as a leader. Have the leader lead the group with a continual pattern of large movements, such as knee slapping, foot stamping or head tapping. The rest of the group needs to watch and follow the leader closely, changing actions as the leader changes without identifying the leader. You can then invite the remaining child to return to the circle and identify the real movement leader. The trick is for the leader to repeat the pattern many times before changing to a new pattern. If the group is very good at following, they can stump the observer.

Repeat the activity so that all students have a turn at a role.

Extending the Activity: You can ask the leader to lead with a repeated pattern rather than with a simple movement. For example, the pattern might be clap, clap, stamp stamp stamp. This keeps the class on their toes as they will have to concentrate hard on following the pattern. It also makes it difficult for the leader to change patterns.

Playing with AB Form

To involve students with the exploration of form, you could introduce this composition activity. As students work in small groups, they will develop their skills to identify, organize and synthesize movement and rhythm to present a product.

You will need to identify a round song. "Row, Row, Row Your Boat" works well, but you may have another favourite round song in your classroom that the children would enjoy. To begin the activity, review the chosen song and teach a movement sequence. The movement sequence should have two distinct parts, just as the round song has two parts: A (Row, row...) and B (Merrily...). The AB form is a combination of two rhythmical and movement patterns. Students joined in as I led them, our arms joined, in swaying side to side for section A and in twirling on the spot for section B.

Invite students to form groups to create their own two movement sequences. You should remind the class that their movements should correspond rhythmically to the pattern and the length of their verse. For the A section, one of my groups developed a stylized rowing movement involving the whole body rocking forward and backward supported by hands and knees. For the B section, another group of students stretched high and gradually lowered themselves down to their hands and knees.

Once each group has refined and rehearsed their section, you might want to invite them to put the movements and song together. The first time through children can dance and sing simultaneously. Later, you could challenge them to repeat the sequences in a round. The visual effect is stunning!

Creating Variations on a Theme

Patterns and variations in words and music provide a great source of learning experiences for children. As students explore and combine the patterns, they develop organizing, interpreting, sequencing and producing skills.

As you prepare for this activity, select a class pattern book. *Charlie Parker Played Be Bop* by Chris Raschka is a wonderful book for this activity. Although it is simple to read, the patterns and variations that are introduced provide some interesting opportunity for exploration for all levels.

Now, invite students to identify a repeating pattern sentence in your chosen book. In our case, "Charlie Parker played Be Bop" was the obvious choice. With the class, talk about the length of the chosen sentence and have them listen to the sentence's beat as you read it. Then, each student should work individually to create a movement sequence for that sentence. Although the sequences will vary, they should all be the same length. You might want to take some time for children to share their sequences with a friend and talk about the interesting points of each sequence. In my classroom, one child tried to capture the travel of sound, beginning with a large wide shape, bursting through space and changing shape as he ran and slowly stopped in a small wide shape.

Returning to the book, ask the students to select two of the pages that appealed to them. Challenge students to create a movement sequence for both pages, beginning with the sequence developed earlier for the chosen sentence. They should somehow base the two new sequences on the original sequence. In my class, one sequence became a wide shape moving low to the ground, then traveling low through space with a slow stop down on the floor. Once students each have three movement sequences, the original and two variations, they are ready to put them all together.

The original sequence now becomes the chorus movement during the sentence and the variation movements represent changes and expansions of the chorus. Once the children have rehearsed all sequences and are familiar with the pages that inspired their two new phrases, they are ready for the finale. Read the book and invite all students to move through their original sequences as they hear the sentence and to perform their own sequences as their selected pages come up. The result: A theme and variation creation!

Across the Curriculum

• Drama: Pantomiming a story

Students can select a character from a known story, such as Peter and the Wolf. Then, you can challenge them to isolate words and actions for their character and put on a silent play, telling about the events through movement only.

• Music: Notating rhythmic patterns

Students can work with rhythm instruments such as lummi sticks, drums, bells, and maracas to create a rhythmic pattern. Then, they can record their pattern on paper with coloured pencils, using symbols such as circles, shapes and lines. You might want to keep a collection of the recorded rhymes and create a class book.

Students can also access recorded instrumental and vocal music to listen for rhythmic patterns. They can listen for long and short sounds and for the overall pattern, and record the patterns on paper.

• Visual Art: Piecing rhythm together

Students can collect pictures in magazines and books that feature a pattern. They can make mosaics by cutting small squares of coloured paper and gluing the paper pieces in a colour pattern on paper. For a textured effect, they could cut the mosaic squares out of several materials, such as glossy paper, coloured paper, foil, wallpaper, and acetate.

• Language Arts: Finding patterns in books

Let students explore pattern books in the classroom language arts program. Gather together a text set of pattern books and immerse students in them for awhile. Soon they will be comparing the patterns in each book and creating their own pattern books.

74

• Math: Manipulating patterns

There are countless math manipulatives that can be used to explore patterns in our world. Students can pattern common classroom materials, such as pattern blocks and building blocks, according to colour, size, shape. . . They enjoy recording their own patterns using noodles, beans and other objects and can challenge one another to try to continue their patterns.

• Physical Education: Playing with rhythm

Small physical education equipment, such as bean bags and rhythm balls, provide some wonderfully clear chances to develop rhythm patterns. You can have students create repeated patterns on their own, working with a ball or bean bag, and listen to the sound pattern created. For example, while working with a ball, "bounce and catch and throw and catch, dribble round and round" creates a wonderful sound pattern on the floor.

7 Working with Elements of Visual Design

Marks on paper can have many meanings. A dash suggests something to come, a period states stillness, and large, bold print yells at the reader. Letters and symbols have been used effectively to record the spoken word and to communicate thoughts and ideas for hundreds of years. Laban and Benesh notation symbols are used to record movement on paper. A full system of notes is used to preserve music for generations to come.

All of these recording techniques draw on elements of art, such as colour, shape and line, to capture a thought, evoke an emotion or record an idea. Lines can take us into and through a work of art, while shape and direction can evoke emotion. Soft curves and rounded shapes appearing on canvas can calm us. Taken all together, the visual features on a piece of paper or canvas can invite and direct the eye to move constantly, affecting the observer in some surprising ways.

Movement brings life to recording techniques that rely on design elements. Red becomes large and vibrant when interpreted through movement, while a circle creates a feeling of breadth as arms and legs extend and wrap around the body. Movement provides art with a three-dimensional appearance and physical meaning.

This chapter enables students to learn skills pertinent to the study of fine arts, such as music, dance and visual design. In it students explore elements of visual design through movement and capture the movements using a variety of recording techniques. Students will respond to colour and line and create and record patterns and pathways. They will map, experiencing floor designs with the body and then recording the experience in a movementscape. They will also create and then move through a legend, and invent movement from a grid. They can apply the skills they learn in this chapter to fine arts, such as music, dance and visual design.

I have done all these activities with primary level students, but you may find it most appropriate to introduce them at the junior level and above.

Exploring Elements of Design

Colours

This colour response activity helps students attend to detail and critically analyze the elements of design in illustrations.

Color Dance by Ann Jonas captures swathes of colour across the page, fabric moving in the hands of dancers. This book has served me as a source of simple colour illustrations and as a stimulus for movement, although many other children's picture books would work. You can begin your movement exploration by having students respond to the colours featured on the pages of your selected book. Students will readily respond to red with vibrant, large movements and to blue with calm, flowing movements. After you have explored a range of colours, you'll need to look a little deeper.

As you revisit each of the book's pages, you might want to ask students some of the following questions:

- What levels is the design on?
- What direction does the design move in?
- Are the lines sharp or smooth?
- How do the colours affect you? Do they make you feel like moving slowly or quickly?
- Does the colour move fast or slowly?

Working with the class, consider each page briefly, taking into consideration the listed questions. Invite students to answer the questions through movement. Their responses should reflect their moving from the middle level to the low and high levels and to levels in between. Similarly, their movements should expand to add backward, sideways and diagonal to the automatic response of forward motion. The tempo and flow of the movement can also change, punctuated by stops and starts and changing from fast to slow.

Lines

Students can use lines to communicate ideas. In this game, they will learn about the variety of lines in the environment and the different forms that lines can take.

Using a book or part of the environment as a reference, have students generate ideas about the large variety of lines in the environment. *The 13th Clue* by Ann Jonas provides a sample of some of the ways that lines can be used to communicate ideas. You may well spark a lively discussion about lines.

This activity requires the use of a gym or a room with lines; however, a tiled floor would do. Ask the children to move around the room on the lines. As students encounter each new line, challenge them to use a new traveling action. Doing this will generate new movements and the frequency of the lines and changes will surprise students. As the children explore lines, you might choose to present one of the following challenges:

- travel off of the lines;
- travel across lines;
- zigzag along the lines;
- combine two lines and maintain the traveling action.

Then, students can leave the floor markings and create their own movement lines on the floor. Using the structure of a movement phrase, students can create a start shape, a traveling action along a line and an end shape.

The resulting movement phrases are far from simple. Many of my students chose to travel along a complex pattern of lines, intertwining zigzag, straight and spiral lines as they traveled through their movement phrase. When the students travel through their phrases simultaneously, they will cover the room with lines.

Filling Space with a Partner

Exploring Floor Patterns

To encourage students to explore lines in the environment with a partner, you might want to suggest this drawing game. The children will learn about the nature and form of lines by representing them in movement with partners and recording line patterns on paper.

Refer to *Lines* by Philip Yenawine, a publication of the Museum of Modern Art, New York. The book addresses lines within art work using simple vocabulary and makes direct references to famous paintings. Now, select a book from your collection and work with your students to make a list of observed lines, and the media used. Your list may include

- straight lines
- curved lines
- zigzag lines
- looping lines
- lines forming shapes

- brushes
- pens
- crayons
- pencils
- fingers

Invite your students to represent each type of listed line through movement without touching anyone else. Each child will likely use a different type of traveling action at a distinct pace and with a unique level of energy. Then, ask the children to explore different widths of lines by imagining that the zigzag line was made thick and even by a brush, thin and scrawny by a fountain pen, light by a pencil, and thick with an uneven texture by a finger.

Once students have explored these lines through movement, invite them to record their pathway on paper. For some this will mean recalling the patterns created and recording them on mural paper. Others may choose to place their paper on the floor and record the pattern as they move; still others may choose to attach the paper to the wall and record as they move.

We continued with this activity into partner work. One partner became responsible for moving along the desired line, while the other partner recorded. Students can change their roles several times. I found it interesting to allow dialogue among partners and to see how they recorded features such as the level, weight or tempo of the movement.

Filling the Space

To allow children to explore the use of space in illustrations and their own environment, you can introduce this drawing and moving activity. Pairs of students will fill paper with lines and designs and then bring their illustrations to life.

All picture book illustrations use space. Many illustrators employ an interesting combination of full page and partial page pictures, borders, line and design to capture story images. Two primary picture books that specifically outline pathways of travel are *The Runaway Duck* by David Lyon and *Rosie's Walk* by Pat Hutchins. You might begin by reviewing with the class a book that features "filled space." Both of these sources gave us a good starting point for filling space.

Filling space begins with pairs of students assigned to an empty working space and a piece of chart or mural paper. Ask each pair to fill their paper with a variety of lines and designs. Some of the designs used might be a star, a diamond, a cross, and an oval, and some of the lines might be dotted, dashed, thick and solid, and thin and squiggly. Ask students to find a beginning point on the paper. Then, challenge the children to bring the lines and spaces to life with movement by traveling along the pathways outlined by lines, whether the lines are simple or combined to form shapes or designs.

I found it necessary to caution students to leave blank space for rest points. This helped to encourage them to do a good job on the lines that they depicted and to some extent avoid the tendency to just fill the space.

Extending the Activity: You can have the partners return to their paper records and decide upon stillness points, steps and shapes along the pattern. Some students, once they have moved along their pattern once, may choose to move simultaneously with partners, while others may choose to move the same way at the same time but in a different part of their space. Still others can move one after the other as if following the leader.

Making Maps, Devising Dances

Designing Movementscapes

You can encourage the children to explore lines and designs with this mapping activity, through which they will learn about mapping techniques.

Choose a book that chronicles travel. The story *Malcolm's Runaway Soap* by Jo Ellen Bogart chronicles the journey of Malcolm's soap as it slips out of his hand and out of his house. The image of the soap's extensive travels helped a group of primary students to get started on a movementscape, while junior-aged students responded to following the stars in *Follow the Drinking Gourd* by Jeanette Winter and *The Drinking Gourd* by F. N. Monjo. You might choose to use any of these three books or another one from your own collection.

Before you read the selected story, give each student a piece of paper and ask them to sketch the path of travel outlined in the story as it is read. The mapping method will vary: some students will use lines and designs to do the mapping, while others will draw pictures of places, objects or events in the story.

The fun begins once students have recorded the patterns of movement. Ask the children to work in groups to travel along each created pattern, responding with movement to the patterns and symbols on the paper. You might want to select an orchestra leader in each group to direct the group members through each pattern.

Once all of the groups have traveled the paths of their members, ask students to join all of their travel paths together to form a collage. You can invite each group leader to direct students along their travels by setting the pace and determining the sequence of movement. The children should have time to practise their movementscapes before they are invited to share their creations with the class.

Extending the Activity: Students can record their travel paths on asphalt with sidewalk chalk. However, some students will still copy the pattern onto paper so that they can return to their travel paths again and again.

Making Movement Maps

Students become involved in creating a movement legend in pictorial form. They will learn about symbols, representation and mapping techniques as they work in groups to make their own legend.

A pictorial reference, such as an atlas or map collection, will help to review mapping techniques. I found that *Three Days on a River in a Red Canoe* by Vera B. Williams provided my class with some good ideas of how to represent places, events and people in pictorial form. With the class, make a list of the symbols and what they represent. Your final list might include these symbols:

LEGEND

Representing	Symbol
Start:	Green circle
Finish:	Red circle
Direction:	Arrow (also used to show change)
Floor pattern:	Arrow in black ink
Air pattern:	Arrow in red ink
Travel:	Solid line
Stillness/pause:	Circle of white
Sequence/order:	Numbers
People:	Initials
Walk:	- - - - - -
Skip:	__-__-__
Run:	-----------
Leap:	__ __ __
Twist:	{ } { } { }
Turn:	∿∿∿

To begin the game, provide each group with a piece of paper and ask the groups to plan their movements on the paper. The children should fill the paper with the plan, using the identified symbols for their mapping. Once the map is complete, have the groups try their own movement legend, using the movement type, direction, and shapes and pauses as recorded.

Once all groups have had an opportunity to create, select and refine their movements, you can put all of the papers together. Try taping each paper back together to form a large whole sheet and post the paper for all to see. You can invite one group at a time to travel through their map to create a moving class map!

Extending the Activity: You might want to add other aspects of movement to the class legend, such as the speed of movement, movement themes and motifs, and changes in direction, level or size. You could even find a way to note accented movements. The children can then add these symbols to their movement maps, adding details and increasing the texture of their maps.

Making Chance Dances

To encourage students to explore movement design, you could introduce the following game of chance. Students will work as a class to invent movement sequences by rolling dice. Once the sequences are joined together, the whole class will have a Chance Dance.

To begin, create a grid and place the categories of movement onto it that have been discussed throughout this chapter. Those categories included colours, actions, lines, and designs/formations.

Then, within each column, ask the children to place the symbols that have been used in earlier activities of this chapter. Your finished grid might have the following information:

	Colours	Actions	Lines	Designs/Formations
1.	yellow	running	thick	diamond
2.	green	leaping	dotted	circular
3.	brown	twisting	angular	octagon
4.	purple	hopping	straight	cross
5.	orange	skipping	uneven	triangle
6.	pink	galloping	spiral	square
7.	blue	walking	wavy	star
8.	grey	turning	thin	oval
9.	white	jumping	round	rectangle
10.	black	other	zigzag	linked

Setting up the chart with numbers down the margin is important. You might want to reproduce and use the chart provided above.

Now the real rolling begins! Invite the children to form groups and provide one dice for each group. Ask one representative from each group to roll the dice to select activities from the created grid. The dice can be passed around the group so that each member rolls and chooses an element from a different column.

Ask the students to create a movement phrase for their chosen dance elements. In my class, one group rolled 3, 8, 2, 7 or a brown, turning, dotted star. Their created movement phrase featured orderly, calm movements with angular changes of direction at the corners of the space.

Once all groups are ready, you can use the dice once again to determine which group will present first and which will follow. Encourage students to rehearse the final piece several times. You might even choose to set the Chance Dance to prerecorded music.

Across the Curriculum

- **Language Arts: Recording stories through chalk talks and story mapping**

Students can jot images, words and pictures on the chalk board as they tell a story. They can thereby plan their storytelling and see the order of events. They can also map a story or focus on the flow and connections between story events in this way.

Students can also use an overhead acetate to map the events in a story. You might ask students to draw a map from left to right showing the order of events with pictures and the people and places involved. Or, you could have others use images in a flow-chart fashion, highlighting the causes and effects of events in a book. Once students have recorded their story map on an overhead acetate, they can place the acetate on the overhead and use the map as a reference as they tell the story.

- **Writing: Using symbols to write rebus stories**

Students can pepper their writing with symbols in the place of words. The use of symbols such as a human eye for the word *I* or an addition sign to represent the word *and* are just a few to begin with. Many students get very involved with rebus stories, in some cases even creating their own symbols and adding a legend at the bottom of their story.

- **Visual Art: Recording on murals, banners and wall
  hangings**

Students can create murals, banners and wall hangings in
response to many of the activities in this chapter. You can assign
each a section of the mural or banner to work on, or have each
group take a section. A greater variety of pictures will result if
students are encouraged to add to any part of the mural. Also,
students can record some of their symbols, colours and design
records from earlier activities right onto the large mural. Taken
all together, you would have a design collection.

- **Music: Recording sounds with symbols**

Students can map music just as they have been mapping movement and events. Starting with a familiar song, such as "Happy
Birthday" or "O Canada," students can work in groups to represent the tune with symbols. They will enjoy thinking of other
tunes to represent and trying to stump their classmates.

- **Media: Projecting stories on the overhead and in slides**

Students can put objects on an overhead to tell a story. They can
manipulate material forms, such as felt figures, as well as small
objects. As the figures move across the screen, they can tell the
story.

   You can purchase blank slides at your local photography store
and have students create pictures, images and designs on the
slides. They can then project the slides as they tell a story, or
project them as a backdrop for movement or drama presentations.

- **Physical Education: Making shapes and symbols with the
  body**

Working in partners and eventually small groups, students enjoy
the challenge of creating numbers, letters, shapes and symbols
with their bodies. Letters such as *O* and *Y* are easy to begin with.
Once students are warmed up, you can invite them to work in
threes to create letters, in fours to create words and as a class
to create a sentence.

8 Determining and Designing Spatial Relationships

The human body moves in time, through space, with effort and in relationship. Space is the place immediately around the body and the general area extending away from the body. The use of levels, directions, air and floor patterns are all elements of space. Students must develop their spatial awareness in order to move effectively in our environment and to identify or determine the spatial relationships among objects.

Spatial design and planning matter greatly to the effective creation of movement in space. Space must be defined for the dancer, and each defined space elicits a different movement response. As students plan their use of space, they become more aware of the many movement possibilities. Students can vary dance design by changing the area of the movement; the angle, space, and texture of the surface; or the relationship of one body to another.

Body shape and symmetry constitutes another visible aspect of space. Symmetry involves dividing space into two balanced portions, evoking an equal feeling. The use of symmetrical shapes and movements creates a sense of balanced activity, tension and energy. On the other hand, asymmetrical shapes and movements suggest inequality and imbalance.

Working through this chapter will help students develop spatial awareness and a knowledge of design. They can readily apply these understandings to fine art design. They can also use them to further mathematical and scientific learning experiences in such areas as mass; calculations of area and perimeter; design in reference to technology, for example, levers and pulleys; patterns in the environment; and even gravity.

Students will plan and design movement, completing choreography exercises. By manipulating movement and discussing the changes, they can develop their understanding of the relationships between space and shape. Chapter activities focus on the exploration of symmetrical and asymmetrical movement and elements and aspects of spatial design.

Starting with the Body

Creating Shapes

For this space-exploring activity you'll need a series of flash cards with shapes on them. With the class, discuss shapes and have the children create a shape card for each idea shared. Then, ask students to scatter about the room as you hold up a shape card. Challenge students to create the displayed shape with their own bodies and to hold the shape until the next card is shown. You can repeat the process with all of the shape flash cards. Then, with the class make a list of descriptors for the created body shapes. Your list might include:

- round
- flat
- pointed
- thin
- irregular
- deep
- thick
- massive
- curved
- jagged
- long

I found it interesting that many students had very different body shapes for any one flash card. This led us to a discussion about the similarities and differences of body shapes and helped us to add detail to our body shape list. The children discovered more and more shapes, making shapes on different levels and using a wider range of body parts. Many of my students then chose to create and display new shape cards.

Extending the Activity: You can ask students to move around the room to music. Challenge them to use different traveling actions and freeze in a suitable shape when they see a shape card. You might want to invite students to move in the given shape until you display the next shape card.

Playing with Physical Form

Sculpting Shapes

Students can explore sculpting and sculpture through the following game. As they work in pairs, students learn to cooperate by sculpting each other into shapes.

To prepare students for this activity, you may choose to examine shapes and sculpture in the environment. Alternatively, you might want to select a book that shows interesting forms, such as *Where the Forest Meets the Sea* by Jeannie Baker. With the class, examine the shapes and make a list of the observed shapes from the sculpture source you choose. You can expand this list by generating discussion about the attributes of the shapes: the space covered, texture, shape, and energy. Your list may have descriptors such as

- twisted
- stretched
- interconnected
- triangular
- a chair
- a machine
- a house

The fun begins as the children bring the descriptors to life. Ask the children to find partners and identify a sculptor. Once that is decided, ask the non-sculptor to become a blob of clay in the hands of the sculptor. The sculptor should gently move the clay to create an interesting shape. Each shape created should be stable enough to be held for a period of time. Once the sculpture is complete, you can have the sculptor and clay change roles. There are countless possibilities for sculpture, but we had fun with oval, interwoven, and connected shapes.

Extending the Activity: Students can also work in pairs to jointly create a sculpture. Have the sculptor begin to sculpt, and invite the "clay" to identify the object being sculpted. The clay can then help to finish making the object and the pair can begin using it through mime. One sculptor in my classroom made a snow ball, which in turn the partners threw back and forth and then built upon to make a snowman. You may find that you need to have pairs jointly decide on an object before it is sculpted and played with.

Experiencing Body Symmetry/Asymmetry

This follow-the-leader activity allows students to physically experience symmetrical and asymmetrical shapes. As partners participate, they will learn to take direction from a peer and to stay on task as matching and mismatching shapes.

The world around us is filled with symmetrical and asymmetrical shapes. With the class, take some time to examine the classroom environment for samples of both types of shapes. You might even challenge students to try to re-create some of the shapes with their bodies. Be sure to discuss the balance of symmetry and the off-balance irregularity of asymmetry.

Invite the children to form pairs and to identify a leader within each pair. Ask the leaders to take a body shape and have the partner match that shape. Encourage leaders to alternate symmetrical and asymmetrical shapes. You can have students change roles and repeat this matching game several times.

Then, make the following challenge. Ask the leader to take balanced, symmetrical shapes and the follower to take an asymmetrical shape for each of the leader's symmetrical shapes. For one group in my class this meant that the follower created the symmetrical start shape, but stretched one arm downwards on a diagonal angle, creating an imbalance. Students can continue creating shapes based on their partners' shapes, focusing on balance, shifting of weight and the use of the space right around the body.

Extending the Activity: You might want to introduce students to positive and negative shaping. Have the leaders create shapes but leave empty spaces within the shapes; ask the followers to fill those spaces. I found it interesting to see the empty space created in rounded and angular bodies with arms and legs sticking through holes and spaces.

Other shape challenges include making

- a big shape with a little shape inside;
- a smooth, slow shape, with the other filling the holes with three sharp shapes;
- a negative shape made by one while the partner makes a shape in, over, through and around, above, below or beside that shape with a hole.

These explorations can result in interesting interconnected shapes.

Relating in Space

To encourage the children to explore spatial relationships between people, you can introduce this partner activity.

You might begin by reviewing with the class the spatial relationships of the classroom. Make a list of the relationships you find. Your final list might include

- in front
- behind
- above
- below
- around
- on

Challenge students to explore ways to travel in relationship with their partners. Invite them to move with one in front and the other behind, one moving high as the partner moves low, and so on. Once the children have explored each of your listed relationships, they should create a movement phrase based on two or more of the relationship words. For one pair in my room, this meant gliding and weaving in semi-circles around each other in a line, one in front and the other behind.

You might choose to change the task by limiting one partner to movement in the space right around the body, while the other partner moves throughout the room. This can continue for sixteen counts before students change their roles. For a pair in my classroom, one partner moved in personal space using small, quick movements, while the other used large and reaching movements to cover the space.

I found that the space limitation really changed partner creations, causing students to work with contrasting spaces, in many ways filling more of the available space. You can have the students alternate their spaces, so that they both work specifically with general and personal space to revisit the movement phrase already developed. For a final challenge, you might ask students to take the basic movement phrase which they have created and focus on changes to level and direction.

Extending the Activity: You can challenge students to create spirals. Have students start by joining hands in a big circle. Designate a student to drop one hand clasp and move around to make a spiral. Meanwhile, the other person with a broken hand clasp should stay still as students follow the leader around and around. Once the spiral is created, students can unfold the spiral by following the centre person as they move through people's legs. You can have the children repeat the process several times to allow several students the chance to lead a spiral.

Combining Bodies, Designing with Shapes

Moving in Shapes

In this activity, students work in groups to create directed shapes. Doing so will help them to develop skills in cooperation and communication.

You might begin by having small groups create a triangle with their bodies. You can challenge them to travel to you in the triangle shape, and then assign a new group shape for them to create. Your shape challenges might include the following:

- a circle without the use of eyes
- a square, but with only three people connected
- a long, thin shape with elbows joined
- a twisted shape on the ground

Having students do this activity without talking, forcing them to really use their eyes, extends the fun. At first, watching this is hilarious: groups generally do not consider the need to allow for traveling. But afterwards, the children should begin to plan ahead of time how their designs will travel.

Making Physical Constructions

In groups, students can work together to construct machines and objects with their bodies. In the process they will develop important skills in cooperation.

Select a factual book or magazine on architecture and buildings. I have found that *What It Feels Like to Be a Building* by Forrest Wilson captures the physical experience of structures, relating building blocks to bodies. Working with your class, discuss the structural functions of physical design and how human bodies can recapture that structure. You might want to invite students to experience with their bodies a small human pyramid with a wide base at the bottom, the bend within a beam and the squeeze

on the bricks within a dome. In the process, students will discover aspects of structural design that lead to far more interesting construction.

Once students are organized into groups, invite them to identify an object that they can re-create with their bodies. Again with
your class, identify objects that can be re-created with the human
body. Your students might list a dishwasher, house duct cleaner,
vacuum cleaner, and new machine to do household chores.

Now for the real challenge. Ask groups of children to select
an object from the list and then work to re-create that object with
their bodies. In my classroom, one group selected the dishwasher,
with four bodies interconnecting on different levels, one person
lifting the plates, the next spraying the plates, the next flipping
the plates and the final person drying the plates.

Alternately, choose a specific household or community area
that is relevant to current classroom studies. When working on
a community topic, I selected the laundromat and asked each
group to construct a new-age machine to replace machines now
used in laundromats.

To add depth to their physical constructions, you might want
to challenge students to consider the following:

- How can you make your machine travel?
- What about the cleaning and maintenance of your machine?
- Are the parts of the machine interdependent?
- What happens when only one person moves?
- How does that affect the rest of the people in the machine?

Designing Dance into Space

This group dance activity encourages students to explore elements
of spatial design in the world around them. Students will learn
the selection, analysis and evaluation skills involved in the design
process.

Design and creation is a fascinating topic for students to explore.
We started this activity by reading the book *The Magic Fan* by
Keith Baker, a tale of a young Japanese boy, Yoshi, whose job
was to design and build objects. You could review any classroom
book that highlights design. Working with your chosen book,
invite students to discuss the role of planning and the importance
of vision in the design process.

Invite students to form groups and to identify their work space.
Now, invite each group to select one of the following formations:

- a straight line
- being scattered throughout the room
- a semi-circle
- a triangle
- a star

You can now challenge each group to create a movement phrase working with the formation, complete with start position, action on the spot and ending shape. Encourage students to explore movement of their arms and legs or they may focus solely on traveling in the formation. Let the groups practise and refine their phrases by repeating them several times and cleaning up the shapes and actions.

When they are ready, ask each group to present their phrase and repeat it. With each repetition of the movement phrase, students should project the movement into space with greater intensity and extension. The movement phrases will become more stretched and reaching, gathering momentum, speed and sharpness. The spatial pattern will remain the same while the effort, rhythm, mood, tempo and parts of the body will introduce changes to the original movement sequence.

Have students repeat their movement phrases, but this time gradually send them into distant space. The movement phrases will cut across space like fingers reaching for an object. For the final section, you might want to have the groups return their phrases to the original form, moving in formation in the immediate space, calm and relaxed.

Extending the Activity: This spatial dimension activity can be used to develop other dances. Students should create a movement phrase that focuses on an element of movement such as shape of movement, shape carved out of the space, or specific timing. In each case, the developed movement phrase should be repeated in a small space, then repeated to fill a wider space, repeated to fill all space, then retracted to the original space.

Across the Curriculum

• Health: Looking at body systems

While studying human systems, students can draw comparisons between human and building systems. They can start by tracing each others' bodies on large pieces of paper. Then they can add details, mapping out their body systems right on the paper. Next, students can draw similarly proportioned pictures of buildings and their electrical, mechanical and ventilation systems. These pictures allow students to look at the similar functions and purposes of the two systems.

• Science: Recording in an inventor's journal

Just as students identify and then solve movement design problems as are presented in this chapter, they can solve problems in many other curriculum areas. Students can use an inventor's journal as a place where they react to thoughts and ideas about problem solving and inventing. They can record their thoughts incidentally, or in response to questions such as "What do you think an invention is?" or "How is invention different from discovery?" Students can also make a list of all the things in the classroom that someone had to invent. Of course, the inventions listed could provide source material for other dance designs.

• Visual Art: Sculpting with wire, paint and material

You might give your students the opportunity to use wire to create and express their ideas. Children can staple a piece of wire to a block of wood or Styrofoam. Then they can twist and turn the wire to sculpt a form then outline the shape of something they would like or make the wire portray some way a person could feel.

Students can apply water-soluble paint in designs on body parts or on sets. Markings on body parts can provide interesting visual effects as the body moves, while painted sets provide an interesting background for movement. Draping material on top of the heads of dancers, around the neck, behind legs, and over the shoulders also enhances sculptural design.

• Language Arts: Creating design books

Students can make shape and colour books to collect pictures of objects of different shapes and colours, and see how those objects appear in art work and in the environment. A design book with sections on shape, colour, formation and design will help students to record their discoveries and to design creations on paper for re-creation later.

• Mathematics: Building structures

Many of the manipulative materials used in math class lend themselves to structural explorations. Materials such as blocks and LEGO can form the basis of exploration for structural design. You might want to introduce books on architectural design and building construction near blocks, so the students can try to re-create the described patterns and designs.

9 Using Props to Explore Societal Issues

The aim of this chapter is to identify and use ideas from the arts to better understand society. If we expect our students to become concerned and contributing citizens, then we must encourage them to consider different perspectives. Movement provides us with a wonderful opportunity to view society from another perspective and to communicate our own responses to societal issues.

Movement can effectively capture these images that we perceive in our surroundings while allowing us to communicate and express our thoughts in response to those images. Movement itself is a system for thinking, a way for us to add information to our knowledge base, a way to represent thoughts and ideas.

Props can extend the expressive and communicative nature of movement. Props such as chairs can be used to extend movement onto new surfaces and structures. Other props, such as poles, handkerchiefs, skirts, books and abstract objects, can be used to stimulate movement. This chapter calls upon students to use props and movement to respond creatively to societal issues that are relevant to the study of drama, social studies, environmental studies and language arts. Students can portray their own vision of societal issues.

Students will explore props, dress up and do paper sculpture. They'll extend movement through puppetry. Working in groups, students will explore movement using dancing sticks, glasses and story shawls. They will also create headdresses and then explore movement possibilities. Throughout the chapter, students can look at the world from other perspectives and respond to the images that they perceive.

Exploring Props

Dressing Up

Dressing up with clothes and objects is a great way to promote dramatic improvisation and movement. As an activity, dressing up has traditionally been limited to students' early years, but it is enjoyable for many youngsters. As students explore the dress-up box, they will learn about character and the influence of clothing and facial expression on people around them.

Few children need an introduction to dress up. Kathy Stinson has captured some of the wonder and fascination that children have with dressing up in her book *The Dressed Up Book*. You might begin by discussing clothes, helping children to identify different ways that they can dress up. Your discussion might include these aspects:

- pieces of clothing
- hair pieces
- hats
- noses

- glasses
- scarves
- movement
- shoes

Let students try on pieces from the dress-up box. You'll find that they become more and more elaborately dressed and undergo small adventures in their costumed roles. You might want to invite the children to explore the movement of their characters, particularly any animals.

We created our own combinations of clothes, noses, and footwear, finding what we could in the box, and creating our own where necessary. We tried moving with our funny feet, webbed feet, and high-heeled feet, and laughed and talked about how the costumes made us move, and how they changed our movements.

Giving Paper Shape

Paper is such an exciting medium, with countless possibilities. Students can turn paper into an object and bring it to life, developing the ability to pay attention to detail and fine motor skills as they do so.

You might begin this activity by discussing the many forms and uses of paper in the classroom. There are many commercially available books on paper making and you might introduce one to your students. I found that *The Paper Crane* by Molly Bang sparked a lively discussion about paper sculpture.

After your discussion, challenge students to create an object through paper sculpture. You may want to challenge students to limit their tools to paper and hands, or you may want to introduce scissors as well. Then, ask them to explore ways to re-create the shapes of their objects with their bodies. Students will do so in many different ways.

I introduced *Sadako and the Thousand Paper Cranes* by Eleanor Coerr, about a Japanese girl who dies of leukemia as a result of radiation from an atom bomb. Sadako tried to fold 1,000 paper cranes because of the belief that the gods would make her well if she did. When she died after folding fewer than 650, her classmates did the rest.

Some of my students brought cranes to life. They represented the cranes by balancing on one leg with the other limbs tucked close to the body; others balanced on both legs with arms and necks stretched. All did a magical Crane Dance, leaping and floating through the air.

Extending the Activity: Students might also make such animals as hens, ducks and parrots out of paper. Encourage them to bring each newly created paper sculpture to life through movement.

Playing the game of Statues is another way to reinforce the use of shapes. Students can move to musical accompaniment. Ask them to move freely around the room, and have them stop to form statues when the music stops. As students become more familiar with the game, you can challenge them to become the statue of an object or character, and then move as that character until the music stops and another object is called.

Extending Movement with Props

Presenting Puppets

Puppetry offers students an opportunity to take on roles and explore life events from another perspective. As students engage in puppetry, they will learn about story characters, storyline development and cooperation with a partner.

You can introduce the topic of puppetry in a number of ways. You might want to invite discussion on puppets that students know, have made or have seen on television. I love to use *Why the Willow Weeps*, a story told with hands by Marshall Izen and Jim West, to stimulate dialogue about the appearance and use of puppets and to initiate discussion about the preservation of the environment.

Now, invite students to work with old gloves and socks to create characters. Challenge students to identify different characters that can be made as puppets. Allow the children time to create a chosen character puppet. Once the puppet characters are created, students can work with partners to create a story that explores the interdependence of two creatures. You might want to have students share their stories with the class.

You can challenge students to make their own bodies into puppets. Each child can take on the character of their created puppet. Then, pairs can work together to develop a different story dance. One story in my classroom was about a mouse and a frog, with the students scurrying and hopping respectively, communicating only through sounds and body gestures. Their puppet characters helped to bring form to their dances.

Dancing with Props

The Dancing Stick

The wand, an interesting novelty item, is sometimes used in the gym program to extend the range of body movement. Students can use the wand to create dances, developing decision-making and social skills in the process.

Students can begin by exploring the use of a wand, or length of dowling, to carve the space immediately around their bodies. You might ask students to see how many ways they can move around the wand while still holding it with one hand and then two. By using one stick or wand to join partners, students can make countless movement connections. They can work individually or in pairs to create a movement sequence involving the stick.

Once students have explored and created with the wand, you can introduce the dancing stick. The dancing stick is a special stick, in our case, a wand with a ribbon attached. It can be used in whole-class sharing sessions to keep class members in order and to allow all students to have a turn. You might like to ask students to sit in small groups in a circle to share their created dances. These dances may have been developed during earlier activities or as a result of exploring and creating with the wand.

Pass the stick around the circle. The only person allowed to dance is the one in possession of the stick. I found that at first many of the children chose to pass the dancing stick on, but once they realized just what was involved — a thirty second performance — they wanted to take a turn and dance whenever they were in possession of the stick.

Extending the Activity: Students can also explore the use of the dancing stick while standing up. This use of the dancing stick places emphasis on improvisation: it doesn't really matter how someone moves just as long as the movement continues to flow. Encourage the person with the stick to dance. As each person finishes dancing, you can challenge him or her to move close to another student and pass the wand. Each new person in possession of the dancing stick should respond immediately with movement; there should be a never ending flow of movement within the group.

Glasses

People always want what they don't have, and people without glasses are no exception — they're curious about wearing glasses. This activity gives all students a chance to play with glasses and experience the world from another perspective. In the process, they will develop sensitivity to others and an appreciation of the use of props for developing characterization.

To introduce the topic I read the book *Glasses: Who Needs 'Em?* by Lane Smith. You might choose a favourite story character who wears glasses to generate your discussion. As you talk, challenge students to identify characters that wear glasses. You may even want to venture into the absurd, and identify people, animals or places that could wear glasses. Your character list could include a raccoon; a planet; a dog; a doctor.

You might choose to purchase some pairs of inexpensive plastic glasses and invite students to wear them. Each student can put on a pair of glasses and move as a character from the chosen list.

Ask students to start with slow, careful movements, as if the characters were slightly unsure of their surroundings, or had just come inside on a bright sunny day. Have students explore more confident movements, certain of their goal and direction. Then, divide the children into groups of four.

Invite the groups to make a short dance, using their plastic sunglasses as props. Having them select a theme or scenario first will help direct group creations. Themes chosen in my classroom included three blind mice, a beach party, and wary detectives. Once all groups have created a Glasses Dance, put all of the sections together.

Extending the Activity: Other props, such as umbrellas, canes and hats, could be used for this activity. Your students will happily share their prop ideas.

The Storytelling Shawl

Students benefit from class discussion about culture. As students participate in this storytelling activity, they will learn listening, speaking, sequencing and presentation skills.

You might begin this activity with a discussion of culture, in which you specifically address those cultures and traditions represented by the students in the classroom. *The Black Snowman* by Phil Mendez tells the tale of a *kente*, an African storytelling shawl which when worn brings to the bearer cultural history stories. After you have discussed culture in your classroom, you can identify one object associated with cultural traditions. I chose to introduce a number of shawls into our classroom.

Divide the children into groups and provide each group with the chosen object. Ask the groups to sit in circles and to take turns with the selected object, each member telling a story. In my class, many students did tell stories from their own cultural heritage. Once the object has moved all around a circle, the children can bring it to life with movement.

Now, you can challenge the children to work in groups to create a story in which all members participate. This story may evolve out of the circle activity. Encourage students to discover and use movements to bring their story to life. In my classroom I saw marching, stretching, speaking and joining hands as the children played the movement roles of the characters in their story. I found it interesting that all of the groups included the chosen object as part of their dance, either as a prop or as a costume for one of the characters.

Extending the Activity: A shawl, scarf or any piece of fabric can be used to give rise to movement on its own. Students can hold onto the fabric with one hand and explore movements that can be done under, over and around the fabric while maintaining a hold. These changes give rise to a greater variety of movement creations. Your class might enjoy working with a parachute to explore movement possibilities and playing parachute games!

Dragon Dance

To encourage students to explore cultures represented in the classroom or community, you might want to introduce this costume dance. Students will learn about the nature of tradition and the role played by dance in the Chinese culture.

You might begin this activity by reviewing a book that introduces the Chinese Dragon Dance. The story of *Chin Chiang and the Dragon's Dance* by Ian Wallace captures some of the richness and detail of the Dragon Dance and costume. Once you have read the book to your class, you might let the children create their own dance costumes.

Working with materials such as newspapers, safety pins or tape, large paper bags, crayons, scissors and pieces of fabric, groups of four can create their own animal headdresses. They can design the headdresses to resemble animals such as the dragon, captured butterflies, birds, mice and rabbits.

Once all groups have created a headdress, they should create a simple movement story with a beginning, middle, and end using it. Challenge students to use their headdresses, like kites in some cases, to alter the appearance of the body and the way the body moves. I found that some children had many ideas about the kinds of shapes and movements they could use. Others looked to the animal for ideas on shapes and appropriate movements. The use of a long kite allowed lifted, flowing movements for a dragon, extending the movement of the human body into the air, while the dragon stamped and reared around the room. The results were so spectacular, that we took time to share each group creation, both the headdress and the dance!

Prop Dance

To encourage students to use props for role play and characterization, you can introduce this activity. As the students create a Prop Dance, they will develop social skills through group cooperation, and selection and refining skills.

With the class, make a list of those objects that can be used to extend movement. Your list may include the following:

- elastic bands and different forms of elastic
- stretch fabric
- boxes of all shapes
- drums
- stools or chairs

Invite your students to choose an object from your created list. Group students according to their chosen object. The first job is for students to explore the use of the prop. Encourage the children to explore the chosen material to determine how the prop can be used to extend movement and how it can alter the way that the body can move. You might want to provide chairs so that students have an interesting platform to move in relation to. Elastics held between partners can also be fun, allowing slow, sustained movements apart and sudden snaps back together.

You can also explore the object in terms of shape, texture, design and basic nature. Encourage students to improvise with their objects until the movement evolves. In my class a group working with stretch fabric tried stretching, waving and folding the fabric, but their interesting movement emerged when they acted on the fabric and reacted to it; they lifted as the fabric lifted, reached as the fabric stretched and waved as the fabric rippled.

You might want to suggest that the members of each group develop a movement commentary based on their group findings. In my class the students addressed current topics such as the environment, an upcoming election and food banks, using their explored prop. With both primary and junior, the final movement creations of my students were presented in broken form, a number of related pieces that did not fit together in an organized way, but together created a movement sequence.

Across the Curriculum

• Drama: Prop stories

Students can tell prop stories by adding props to their storytelling. One story that works well is *Stone Soup* by Marcia Brown where they can use an actual stone in the retelling or dramatization. Another, *James and the Giant Peach* by Roald Dahl, can be developed around a large paper mâché peach stone. Also, they can enhance their telling of traditional tales such as Little Red Riding

Hood by clothing, such as a red hood or a lace cap. You might want to introduce a dress-up box in the classroom and encourage students to use and add to the contents of the box. Or, set up a separate prop box and add props that students have made to accompany their drama presentations. Some of the props used in this chapter, for example, a storytelling shawl, dancing stick or sunglasses, would provide a good beginning for your classroom prop box.

• Language Arts: Clothesline stories

Virtually any story can be retold using a clothesline. First, string a clothesline across a section of the classroom. Identify objects from the story and make those objects out of paper or a variety of materials. Once you have created them, you can attach them to the clothesline using clothes pegs as you tell the story. Your students will soon be clamouring for their turn to retell stories by sequencing story objects and events. Students can create their own clothesline stories by gathering and creating props to peg to the clothesline.

• Music: Instrument props

Homemade instruments are wonderful additions to both a prop box and storytelling sessions. Students can put simple materials such as beans or corn into closed toilet-paper rolls or joined paper plates to create rhythm instruments. They can then place the instruments in the prop box or at the storytelling centre and use them as needed.

• Visual Art: Paper sculpture and origami

Illustrators use paper in many different ways while illustrating books. They use it both to frame and create illustrations. You might want to gather together the work of illustrators who incorporate paper in their illustrations and invite students to try some of the techniques used. Paper sculpture is introduced in this chapter through the book *The Paper Crane*. Students enjoy folding, cutting, tearing and gluing paper to form designs and creations. Another use of paper suggested in this chapter is the Japanese art of paper folding, origami. *The Great Origami Book* by Zulal Ayture-Scheele outlines how to create several objects out of paper.

• Physical Education: Prop games

Students can enjoy prop games in the gym. For one, begin with several students on their hands and knees covered by a sheet. The students must try to travel together in the same direction; as they travel, they must remain covered by the sheet. The challenge is to cooperate and communicate so that they can reach their shared goal. Once they do, you can ask students to repeat the activity standing up, in a larger group or supporting several props.

Conclusion

In the past, educators perceived that the benefit of movement was limited to the physical self alone. Movement meant movement in the gym and was tied to athletic prowess, ball skills and physical fitness. The educational system had isolated education of the physical body from cognitive learning and has perpetuated the separation for many years.

As new curriculum guidelines reflect, that has begun to change. *Shake, Rattle and Learn* combines cognitive, affective and psychomotor learning together in a holistic fashion, contributing to the total education of the total child. It should enable you to see, as you combine psychomotor instruction with cognitive and affective instruction across previously created barriers, a carryover in learning that in turn maximizes student learning.

Discover for yourself that movement provides an approach to learning which is concrete and meaningful to children. By working through activities outlined in this book, students will obtain information about themselves and their world and process and respond to that information in a meaningful manner. I myself have found that taking a movement approach into the classroom allows students to gain a very personal way of learning about themselves and the world around them.

Bringing movement into the classroom benefits kinesthetic learners. You will be able to see the different learning styles of students and identify those students who learn through movement. In many cases, those students are the same who have failed to shine under traditional instructional techniques; now they can demonstrate knowledge, skills and attitudes through their movement. These students will also carry over the effects of their positive and satisfying movement-based learning experiences to all components of the school day.

Even students who are not primarily kinesthetic learners will benefit. They will find themselves expanding their learning experiences into another dimension, the physical dimension, and will form new and different understandings as a result of their movement experiences. For many faltering students, the inclusion of movement in the instruction of curriculum will turn around their academic performance and get them moving along a path of success.

Shake, Rattle and Learn offers a beginning point, a trampoline toward a movement approach to learning. As your students begin to learn through movement in the classroom, you'll begin to identify many situations in which movement can enhance classroom learning. You may even discover what contribution movement can make to your own learning, both as a teacher and as a lifelong learner.

The students will have much to contribute. With their learning flourishing and their motivation strong, as I know it will be, they will begin to request that you take a movement approach to other classroom studies. And they will, I'm sure, be happy to suggest ways to do so!

So, let movement break through outer walls and into your classroom. Let movement spark involvement and generate learning. Then, watch for proof of the value of movement-based learning—you'll see movement "ahas" and physical evidence of learning—and shake, rattle and learn with your students!

Resources

Chapter One

Baker, Keith. *Hide and Snake*. New York: Harcourt Brace Jovanovich, 1991.

Bourgeois, Paulette. *Grandma's Secret*. Boston: Little, Brown & Co., 1988. Toronto: Kids Can Press, 1989.

Browne, Anthony. *Changes*. London, U.K.: Walker Books, 1990. New York: Knopf Books for Young Readers, 1991.

Heide, Florence Parry. *The Shrinking of Treehorn*. New York: Holiday House, 1971.

Irvine, Joan. *How to Make Pop-ups*. Toronto: Kids Can Press, 1987. New York: William Morrow & Co., 1988.

Poulin, Stéphane. *Travels for Two: Stories and Lies from My Childhood*. Toronto: Annick Press, 1991. Willowdale, ON: Firefly Books, 1991.

Rosen, Michael. *We're Going on a Bear Hunt*. London, U.K.: Walker Books, 1989. New York: Macmillan Children's Book Group, 1989.

Scieszka, Jon. *The True Story of the Three Little Pigs*. New York: Viking Penguin, 1989.

Van Allsburg, Chris. *The Mysteries of Harris Burdick*. Boston: Houghton Mifflin, 1984.

Williams, Vera B. *Stringbean's Trip to the Shining Sea*. New York: Scholastic Inc., 1990.

Chapter Two

Agee, Jon. *The Incredible Painting of Felix Clousseau*. New York: Farrar, Strauss & Giroux, 1990.

Cleaver, Elizabeth. *The Enchanted Caribou.* Toronto: Oxford University Press, 1985. New York: Macmillan Children's Book Group, 1985.

Dorros, Arthur. *Me and My Shadow.* New York: Scholastic Inc., 1990.

Gile, John. *The First Forest.* Wisconsin: John Gile Communications, 1989.

Mahy, Margaret. *The Boy with Two Shadows.* London, U.K.: J. M. Dent, 1987. New York: HarperCollins Children's Books, 1988.

Tresselt, Alvin. *Rain Drop Splash.* New York: Mulberry Books, 1990.

Van Allsburg, Chris. *The Widow's Broom.* Boston: Houghton Mifflin, 1992.

Chapter Three

Boegehold, Betty D. *The Fight.* New York: Bantam Doubleday Dell Publishing Group, 1991.

Browne, Anthony. *Willy and Hugh.* Vancouver, B.C.: Douglas and McIntyre, 1991. New York: Knopf Books for Young Readers, 1991.

Edwards, Michelle. *Chicken Man.* New York: Lothrop, Lee & Shepard Books, 1991.

Fox, Mem. *Wilfrid Gordon McDonald Partridge.* New York: Kane/Miller Book Publishers, 1985. Harmondsworth, U.K.: Viking Kestrel, 1986.

Leaf, Munro. *The Story of Ferdinand.* New York: Puffin Books, 1993.

Wild, Margaret. *The Very Best of Friends.* Toronto: Kids Can Press, 1990. New York: Harcourt Brace Jovanovich, 1994.

Chapter Four

Fox, Mem. *Night Noises.* San Diego, CA: Harcourt Brace Jovanovich, 1989.

Martin, Bill, Jr., and John Archambault. *Listen to the Rain.* New York: Henry Holt and Company, 1988.

Obligado, Lillian. *Faint Frogs Feeling Feverish & Other Tantalizing Tongue Twisters.* New York: Puffin Books, 1986.

Prelutsky, Jack. *The Headless Horseman Rides Tonight: More Poems to Trouble Your Sleep.* New York: Mulberry Books, 1992.

Williams, Linda. *The Little Old Lady Who Was Not Afraid of Anything.* New York: HarperCollins Children's Books, 1986.

Chapter Five

Blake, Quentin. *All Join In.* London, U.K.: Red Fox Books, 1992.

Dahl, Roald. *Revolting Rhymes.* New York: Puffin Books, 1984.

Fleischman, Paul. *I Am Phoenix: Poems for Two Voices.* New York: HarperCollins Children's Books, 1985.

Fleischman, Paul. *Joyful Noise.* New York: HarperCollins Children's Books, 1992.

Hayes, Sarah. *Stamp Your Feet.* New York: Lothrop, Lee & Shepard Books, 1988. London, U.K.: Walker Books, 1989.

O'Huigin, Sean. *Scary Poems for Rotten Kids.* Windsor, ON: Black Moss Press, 1988. Willowdale, ON: Firefly Books, 1988.

Ormerod, Jan. *Rhymes Around the World.* London, U.K.: Puffin Books, 1985.

Parry, Caroline, Ed. *Zoomerang a Boomerang.* Toronto: Kids Can Press, 1991. New York: Puffin Books, 1993.

Pelham, David. *Worms Wiggle.* New York: Simon & Schuster Trade, 1989.

Rosen, Michael. *Freckly Feet and Itchy Knees.* London, U.K.: HarperCollins, 1990. New York: Doubleday, 1990.

Chapter Six

Cole, Joanna. *Anna Banana: 101 Jump-Rope Rhymes.* New York: Morrow Junior Books, 1989.

King, Karen. *Oranges and Lemons.* Oxford, U.K.: Oxford University Press, 1985. New York: Oxford University Press, 1987.

Martin, Bill, Jr., and John Archambault. *Barn Dance!* New York: Henry Holt and Company, 1986.

Punt, Irene. *The Bop.* Richmond Hill, ON: Scholastic Canada, 1989.

Raschka, Chris. *Charlie Parker Played Be Bop.* New York: Orchard Books, 1992.

Yolen, Jane, Ed. *Street Rhymes Around the World.* Honesdale, PA: Boyds Mills Press, Inc., 1992.

Chapter Seven

Bogart, Jo Ellen. *Malcolm's Runaway Soap.* Richmond Hill, ON: Scholastic Canada, 1988.

Hutchins, Pat. *Rosie's Walk.* New York: Macmillan Children's Book Group, 1968.

Jonas, Ann. *Color Dance.* New York: Greenwillow Books, 1989.

Jonas, Ann. *The 13th Clue.* New York: Greenwillow Books, 1992.

Lyon, David. *The Runaway Duck*. New York: Mulberry Books, 1987.

Monjo, F. N. *The Drinking Gourd*. New York: HarperCollins Children's Books, 1970.

William, Vera B. *Three Days on a River in a Red Canoe*. New York: Mulberry Books, 1986.

Winter, Jeanette. *Follow the Drinking Gourd*. New York: Knopf Books for Young Readers, 1992.

Yenawine, Philip. *Lines*. New York: Delacorte Press, 1991.

Chapter Eight

Baker, Jeannie. *Where the Forest Meets the Sea*. New York: Greenwillow Books, 1988.

Baker, Keith. *The Magic Fan*. San Diego, CA: Harcourt Brace Jovanovich, 1989.

Wilson, Forrest. *What It Feels Like to Be a Building*. Washington, DC: The Preservation Press, 1988.

Chapter Nine

Ayture-Scheele, Zulal. *The Great Origami Book*. New York: Sterling Publishing, 1987.

Bang, Molly. *The Paper Crane*. New York: Mulberry Books, 1987.

Browne, Marcia. *Stone Soup*. New York: Macmillan Children's Book Group, 1986.

Coerr, Eleanor B. *Sadako and the Thousand Paper Cranes*. New York: Putnam Publishing Group, 1993.

Dahl, Roald. *James and the Giant Peach*. New York: Puffin Books, 1988.

Izen, Marshall, and Jim West. *Why the Willow Weeps*. New York: Doubleday, 1992.

McLellan, Joseph. *Nanabosho Dances*. Winnipeg, MB: Pemmican Publications Inc., 1991.

Mendez, Phil. *The Black Snowman*. New York: Scholastic Inc., 1989.

Smith, Lane. *Glasses: Who Needs 'Em?* New York: Penguin Books, 1991.

Stinson, Kathy. *The Dressed Up Book*. Toronto: Annick Press, 1990. Willowdale, ON: Firefly Books, 1990.

Wallace, Ian. *Chin Chiang and the Dragon's Dance*. New York: Macmillan Children's Book Group, 1984. Toronto: Groundwood Books, 1992.

Bibliography

Beatty, Patricia. *Form Without Formula: A Concise Guide to the Choreographic Process.* Toronto: Dance Collection Danse Press, 1994.

Blom, Lynne Anne, and L. Tarin Chaplin. *The Moment of Movement: Dance Improvisation.* Pittsburgh, PA: University of Pittsburgh Press, 1988.

Findlay, Elsa. *Rhythm and Movement: Applications of Dalcroze Eurythmics.* Princeton, NJ: Summy-Birchard Music, 1971.

Grant, Janet Millar. *Creativity in Motion.* Holmes Beach, FL: Learning Publications, 1992.

Grant, Janet Millar. *Moving into Language Arts.* Richmond Hill, ON: Scholastic Canada, 1991.

Hill, Susan. *Games That Work: Cooperative Games and Activities for the Primary School Classroom.* Victoria, Australia: Eleanor Curtain Publishing, 1992. Winnipeg, MB: Peguis, 1992.

Humphrey, Doris. *The Art of Making Dances.* New York: Grove Press, 1987.

North, Marion. *Movement & Dance Education: A Guide for the Primary and Middle School Teacher.* Plymouth, U.K.: Northcote House, reprinted 1990.

Preston-Dunlop, Valerie. *A Handbook for Dance in Education,* Essex, U.K.: Macdonald and Evans, 1980.

Slater, Wendy. *Teaching Modern Educational Dance: Creative Development in the Primary School.* Plymouth, U.K.: Northcote House, reprinted 1990.

Turner, Margery J. *New Dance: Approaches to Nonliteral Choreography.* Pittsburgh, PA: University of Pittsburgh Press, 1976.

Index